FOUNDATION EDITION

OCR GCSE (9–1) HISTORY B (SHP)

THE MAKING OF AMERICA

1789–1900

JAMIE BYROM
ALEX FORD

An OCR endorsed textbook

The Schools History Project

Set up in 1972 to bring new life to history for school students, the Schools History Project has been based at Leeds Trinity University since 1978. SHP continues to play an innovatory role in history education based on its six principles:

- Making history meaningful for young people
- Engaging in historical enquiry
- Developing broad and deep knowledge
- Studying the historic environment
- Promoting diversity and inclusion
- Supporting rigorous end enjoyable learning.

These principles are embedded in the resources which SHP produces in partnership with Hodder Education to support history at Key Stage 3, GCSE (SHP OCR B) and A level. The Schools History Project contributes to national debate about school history. It strives to challenge, support and inspire teachers through its published resources, conferences and website: http://www.schoolshistoryproject.co.uk

This resource is endorsed by OCR for use with specification OCR Level 1/2 GCSE (9–1) in History B (Schools History Project) (J411). In order to gain OCR endorsement, this resource has undergone an independent quality check. Any references to assessment and/or assessment preparation are the publisher's interpretation of the specification requirements and are not endorsed by OCR. OCR recommends that a range of teaching and learning resources are used in preparing learner for assessment. OCR has not paid for the production of this resource, nor does OCR receive any royalties from its sale. For more information about the endorsement process, please visit the OCR website, www.ocr.co.uk

The publishers thank OCR for permission to use specimen exam questions on pages 100–103 from OCR's GCSE (9–1) History B (Schools History Project) © OCR 2016. OCR have neither seen nor commented upon any model answers or exam guidance related to these questions.

The wording and sentence structure of some written sources have been adapted and simplified to make them accessible to all pupils while faithfully preserving the sense of the original.

Every effort has been made to trace all copyright holders, but if any have been inadvertently overlooked, the Publishers will be pleased to make the necessary arrangements at the first opportunity.

Although every effort has been made to ensure that website addresses are correct at time of going to press, Hodder Education cannot be held responsible for the content of any website mentioned in this book. It is sometimes possible to find a relocated web page by typing in the address of the home page for a website in the URL window of your browser.

Hachette UK's policy is to use papers that are natural, renewable and recyclable products and made from wood grown in well-managed forests and other controlled sources. The logging and manufacturing processes are expected to conform to the environmental regulations of the country of origin.

Orders: please contact Hachette UK Distribution, Hely Hutchinson Centre, Milton Road, Didcot, Oxfordshire, OX11 7HH.
Telephone: +44 (0)1235 827827. Email education@hachette.co.uk Lines are open from 9 a.m. to 5 p.m., Monday to Friday.
You can also order through our website: www.hoddereducation.co.uk

ISBN: 978 1 5104 6959 4

© Jamie Byrom, Alex Ford 2019

First published in 2019 by
Hodder Education,
An Hachette UK Company
Carmelite House
50 Victoria Embankment
London EC4Y 0DZ

www.hoddereducation.co.uk

The authorised representative in the EEA is Hachette Ireland, 8 Castlecourt Centre,
Dublin 15, D15 XTP3, Ireland (email: info@hbgi.ie)

Impression number   10 9 8 7 6 5 4

Year   2024

All rights reserved. Apart from any use permitted under UK copyright law, no part of this publication may be reproduced or transmitted in any form or by any means, electronic or mechanical, including photocopying and recording, or held within any information storage and retrieval system, without permission in writing from the publisher or under licence from the Copyright Licensing Agency Limited. Further details of such licences (for reprographic reproduction) may be obtained from the Copyright Licensing Agency Limited, www.cla.co.uk

Cover photo © Prints & Photographs Division, Library of Congress, LC-DIG-ppmsca-40073

Illustrations by Aptara Inc.

Typeset in India by Aptara Inc.

Printed and bound by CPI Group (UK) Ltd, Croydon CR0 4YY

A catalogue record for this title is available from the British Library.

CONTENTS

	Introduction **Making the most of this book**	2
1	Growing pains **What tensions arose as the USA grew, 1789–1838?** *Closer look 1* – Slavery: Hands, fingers and blood *Key idea summary 1* – Causes	8
2	Visions **How did different groups see the American West, 1839–60?** *Closer look 2* – The diary of Abigail Scott *Key idea summary 2* – Consequences	26
3	'A new birth of freedom'? **What sense can be made of the Civil War and its aftermath, 1861–77?** *Closer look 3* – John Brown: Fanatical abolitionist *Key idea summary 3* – Change	44
4	Smoke and blood **Settlement and conflict on the Plains, 1861–77** *Closer look 4* – Picturing Little Bighorn *Key idea summary 4* – Significance	62
5	We the people **How did life in the United States change, 1877–1900?** *Closer look 5* – Quanah Parker: One man, many visions *Key idea summary 5* – Diversity	80
	Preparing for the examination	96
	Glossary	104
	Index	106
	Acknowledgements	108

Introduction

Making the most of this book

Where this book fits into your GCSE history course

The course

The GCSE history course you are following is made up of five different studies. These are shown in the table below. For each type of study you will follow **one** option. We have highlighted the option that this particular book helps you with.

OCR SHP GCSE B

Paper 1 1¾ hours	**British thematic study** • The People's Health • Crime and Punishment • Migrants to Britain	20%
	British depth study • The Norman Conquest • The Elizabethans • Britain in Peace and War	20%
Paper 2 1 hour	**History around us** • Any site that meets the given criteria.	20%
Paper 3 1¾ hours	**World period study** • Viking Expansion • The Mughal Empire • <mark>The Making of America</mark>	20%
	World depth study • The First Crusade • The Aztecs and the Spanish Conquest • Living under Nazi Rule	20%

The world period study

The world period study focuses on a wider world society. It explores the relationship between different cultures at a time of great upheaval.

Introduction

You will be examined on the world period study as part of Paper 3. We give you more advice about the examination on pages 96–103.

Here is exactly what the specification requires for this world period study.

The Making of America, 1789–1900

Sections	Learners should study the following content:
America's expansion, 1789–1838	• How and why the USA expanded, from 1789 to 1838 • The expansion of Southern cotton plantations and of slavery, 1793–1838 • The removal of **indigenous** people from the East, 1830–38
The West, 1839–60	• The culture of the Plains Indians, including a case study of the Lakota Sioux • The journeys of the early **migrants** to California and Oregon; the Mormon settlement of Utah • The nature and impact of the Californian gold rush (1848–49) and the consequences of the Pike's Peak gold rush (1858–59)
Civil War and Reconstruction, 1861–77	• Divisions over slavery and the causes of the Civil War • The African-American experience of the Civil War, 1861–65 • Reconstruction and continuing limitations to African-American liberty
Settlement and conflict on the Plains, 1861–77	• The causes and nature of white American **exploitation** of the Plains: railroads, ranches and cow towns • Homesteaders: living and farming on the Plains • The US–Lakota Sioux including Little Crow's War (1862), Red Cloud's War (1865–68) and the Great Sioux War (1876–77)
American cultures, 1877–1900	• Changes to the Plains Indians' way of life, including the impact of reservations and the destruction of the buffalo • The impact of economic, social and political change on the lives of African Americans • The growth of big business, cities and mass migration

You need to understand:

- how and why American territory expanded, 1789–1900
- the relationship between this expansion and the cultures of Native Americans, African Americans and white Americans.

You need to be able to:

- identify, describe and explain events and developments relating to these three cultures and the conflicts between them in these years.

The next two pages show how this book works.

A note on language

For some of the events and people referred to in this book there are alternative names and terms. In some cases, terms that were previously commonly used, are now used less and are considered offensive by some people.

In this title we have updated the text to use Native Americans or Indigenous people rather than Plains Indians.

We have continued to use 'Little Crow's War', 'Red Cloud's War' and the 'Great Sioux War' as these are widely used, including in the OCR specification. However, some modern historians suggest that we shouldn't call these 'Indian' wars, because it suggests that Native Americans were to blame for starting them, and as will be clear in this book, that was not the case. So we will also refer to alternative names for these wars.

How this book works

The rest of this book (from pages 8 to 95) is carefully arranged to match what the specification requires. It does this through the following features:

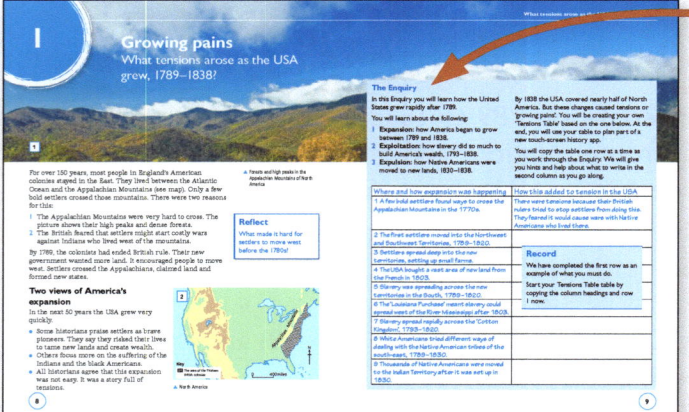

Enquiries

The book is largely taken up with five 'enquiries'. Each enquiry sets you a challenge in the form of an overarching question.

The first two pages of the enquiry set up the challenge. You will find the instructions set out in 'The Enquiry' box, on a blue background, as in this example.

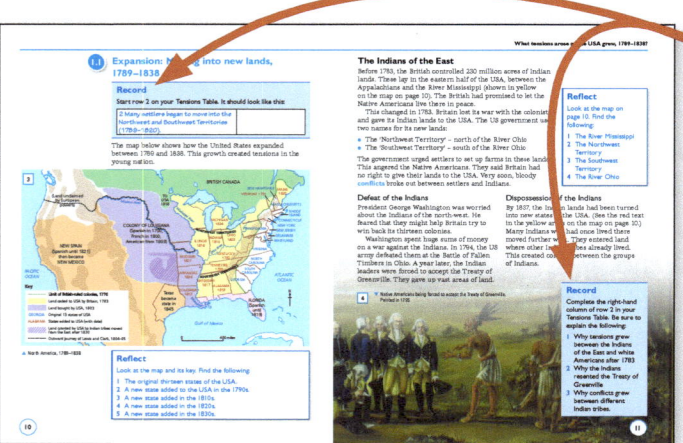

Record

From that point, the enquiry is divided into three or four sections. These match the bullet points shown in the specification on page 3. Each new section starts with a large coloured heading like the one shown here. Throughout each section are 'Record' tasks. These will ask you to record the ideas and information that will help you answer the main question. You can see examples of these 'Record' instructions here.

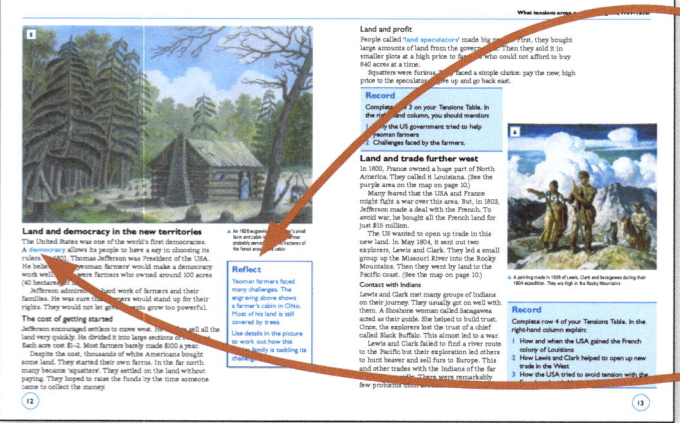

Reflect

At regular intervals we will set a 'Reflect' task. This is to prompt you to think carefully about what you are reading. You do not need to write down the ideas that you get when you do these Reflect tasks. They may still help you when you reach the next Record instruction.

Words in coloured, bold print are explained in the glossary, pages 104–5. You will find other words explained there as well.

Introduction

Review

Most enquiries end by asking you to review what you have been learning. This is where you will answer the main question. All the ideas and evidence that you have gathered will help to support your answer.

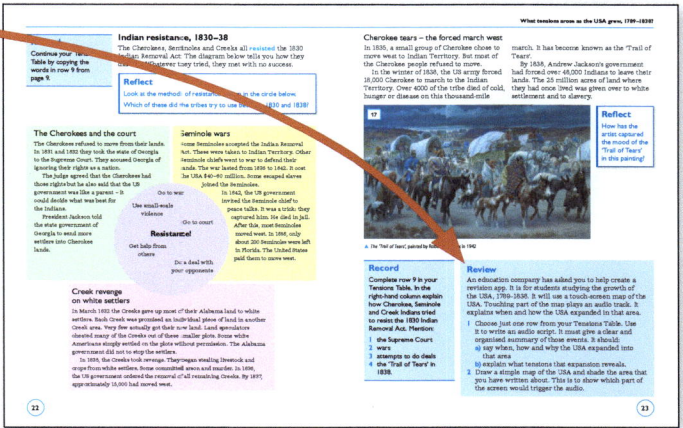

Closer looks and key idea summaries

Between the enquiries are pages that help you in two different ways.

- 'Closer looks' give you a chance to look in more depth at some aspect of the enquiry you have just finished.
- 'Key idea summaries' are about history's big ideas. These ideas (such as cause or consequence) crop up all the time in any period that you study. The summaries consider one key idea from the enquiry you have just finished.

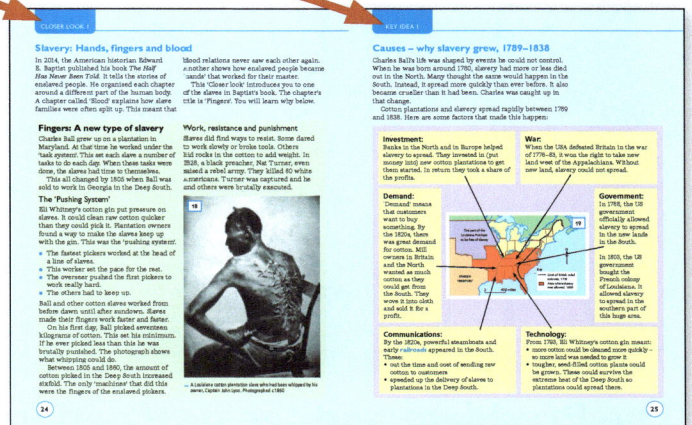

One very important final point

The enquiry questions should help you get to the really important issues in the course. But the examiners will almost certainly ask you different questions when you take your GCSE.

Don't simply rely on the notes you made to answer the enquiry question we gave you. You should make summaries and all sorts of revision notes to prepare for the examination. Pages 96–103 give you lots of advice about this.

You will find that the Record and Reflect tasks also prepare you for the style of questions that you will be asked in the examination. The panel on the right gives you some examples.

- The Reflect task on page 10, for example, would help you with a **Question 1** that asked you to identify one of America's great rivers or mountain ranges.
- The Record task on page 32 would help you to answer a **Question 2**. A 'clear and organised summary' of the movement west of migrants could be based on two or three of the columns in your notes.
- The Record task on page 37 would help you with a **Question 3**. These ask you to explain why something happened or what the impact of an event was.
- The Record tasks throughout Enquiry 3 are very like **Questions 4 or 5** in the exam. Those always ask you to say how far you agree with a given statement.

A new beginning

First in Peace – an engraving made by John C. McRae, c.1866

The President and the new nation

This picture shows George Washington arriving in New York City on 23 April 1789. Cheering crowds have turned out to greet him. He stands and raises his hat to thank them. He was about to become the first ever **President** of their brand new nation: the United States of America (USA).

> **Reflect**
> - Find George Washington in the picture.
> - How has the artist made this look like a moment filled with joy and hope?

It is no surprise that Americans chose Washington as the first leader of the USA. He was the general who had recently won their freedom in a war against Britain. Before this, Americans lived in thirteen British-ruled colonies. They had to follow laws that were made thousands of miles away in the British Parliament.

Then, on 4 July 1776, Washington and other American leaders made their famous 'Declaration of Independence'. This told the British that its old colonies must now be free to rule themselves. The Americans claimed the right to 'Life, Liberty and the pursuit of Happiness'.

This book explores how the USA developed from 1789 to 1900. It may have been searching for liberty and happiness, but the new nation faced many dark and difficult times. The Declaration of Independence promised freedoms but they were not for everyone. Enslaved African Americans and women were not allowed to share in the freedoms. And Indigenous peoples would be forced to give up their lands to make way for the new nation.

Introduction

The new nation and its rules

By 1789, the leaders of the new nation had agreed on a system of government for the USA. Here are some of its main features.

You may want to come back to this page at times as you learn more about how the new nation developed, 1789–1900.

The President
The USA did not want a king. Instead it had a president who looked after matters that affected the whole nation. He was elected every four years. He had to keep to the Constitution.

The Congress
This was made up of people elected from each state. It passed laws. These had to keep to the Constitution.

The Supreme Court
This court heard the nation's most difficult law cases and decided if new laws fitted with the Constitution.

The States
These were areas that were full members of the United States. They could make their own laws so long as these kept to the Constitution. State voters could vote in national elections, e.g. sending **Representatives** to Congress and choosing the President.

The Territories
These were areas with too few people to become a state. The Constitution said a territory could become a state when its population was large enough. Until then, its people could not vote in national elections.

The Constitution
The rules about how the country should be run were written in 'the Constitution'. All the states had to keep to these rules.

The people of the new nation

White Americans
- These Americans came originally from Britain or other parts of Europe.
- Most white males in the USA were allowed to vote.
- Women in the USA could not vote at all.

Native Americans
- These indigenous peoples had lived in North America for thousands of years.
- They belonged to different tribes.
- They could vote if they paid US taxes.

Black Americans
- There were nearly 700,000 African Americans (also called black Americans) in the USA in 1789.
- Most lived as enslaved people in the Southern states.
- Enslaved people could not vote.

Reflect
Which of these groups do you think had fewer rights in America in 1789:
- white women
- Native Americans
- enslaved people?

1 Growing pains
What tensions arose as the USA grew, 1789–1838?

Forests and high peaks in the Appalachian Mountains of North America

For over 150 years, most people in England's American colonies stayed in the East. They lived between the Atlantic Ocean and the Appalachian Mountains (see map). Only a few bold American colonists crossed those mountains. There were two reasons for this:

1. The Appalachian Mountains were very hard to cross. The picture shows their high peaks and dense forests.
2. The British feared that American colonists might start costly wars against Native Americans who lived west of the mountains.

By 1789, the colonists had ended British rule. Their new government wanted more land. It encouraged people to move west. Settlers crossed the Appalachians, claimed land and formed new states.

> **Reflect**
>
> What made it hard for settlers to move west before the 1780s?

Two views of America's expansion

In the next 50 years the USA grew very quickly.

- Some historians praise American colonists as brave pioneers. They say they risked their lives to tame new lands and create wealth.
- Others focus more on the suffering of the Native Americans and the black Americans.
- All historians agree that this expansion was not easy. It was a story full of tensions.

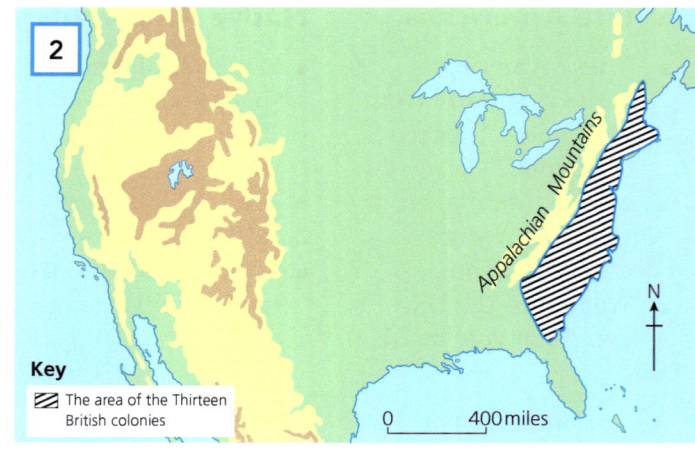

North America

Key: The area of the Thirteen British colonies

0   400 miles

What tensions arose as the USA grew, 1789–1838?

The Enquiry

In this Enquiry you will learn how the United States grew rapidly after 1789.

You will learn about the following:

1 **Expansion**: how America expanded between 1789 and 1838.
2 **Exploitation**: how slavery did so much to build America's wealth, 1793–1838.
3 **Expulsion**: how Native Americans were moved to new lands, 1830–1838.

By 1838 the USA covered nearly half of North America. But these changes caused tensions or 'growing pains'. You will be creating your own 'Tensions Table' based on the one below. At the end, you will use your table to plan part of a new touch-screen history app.

You will copy the table one row at a time as you work through the Enquiry. We will give you hints and help about what to write in the second column as you go along.

Where and how expansion was happening	How this added to tension in the USA
1 A few bold American colonists found ways to cross the Appalachian Mountains in the 1770s.	There were tensions because their British rulers tried to stop settlers from doing this. They feared it would cause wars with Native Americans who lived there.
2 The first American colonists moved into the Northwest and Southwest Territories, 1789–1820.	
3 American colonists spread deep into the new territories, setting up small farms.	
4 The USA bought a vast area of new land from the French in 1803.	
5 Slavery was spreading across the new territories in the South, 1789–1820.	
6 The 'Louisiana Purchase' meant slavery could spread west of the River Mississippi after 1803.	
7 Slavery spread rapidly across the 'Cotton Kingdom', 1793–1820.	
8 White Americans tried different ways of dealing with the Native American tribes of the south-east, 1789–1830.	
9 Thousands of Native Americans were moved to the Indian Territory after it was set up in 1830.	

Record

We have completed the first row as an example of what you must do.

Start your Tensions Table table by copying the column headings and row 1 now.

1.1 Expansion: Colonising new lands, 1789–1838

Record

Start row 2 on your Tensions Table. It should look like this:

| 2 Many American colonists began to move into the Northwest and Southwest Territories (1789–1820). | |

The map below shows how the United States expanded between 1789 and 1838. This growth created tensions in the young nation.

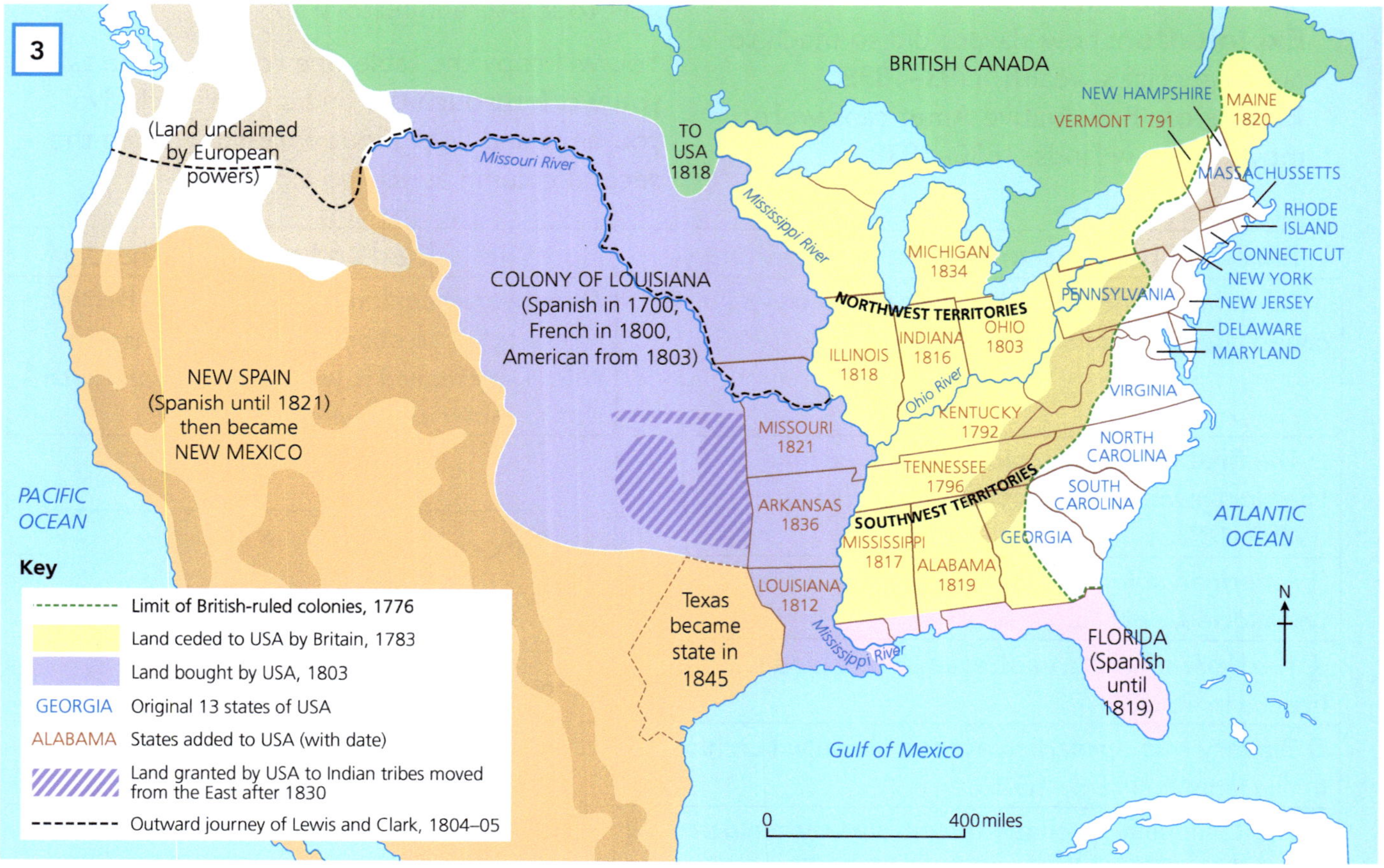

▲ North America, 1789–1838

Reflect

Look at the map and its key. Find the following:

1. The original thirteen states of the USA.
2. A new state added to the USA in the 1790s.
3. A new state added in the 1810s.
4. A new state added in the 1820s.
5. A new state added in the 1830s.

The indigenous peoples

Before 1783, the British controlled 230 million acres of Native American land. These lay in the eastern half of the USA, between the Appalachians and the River Mississippi (shown in yellow on the map on page 10). The British had promised to let the Native Americans live there in peace.

This changed in 1783. Britain lost its war with the colonists and gave occupied Native American territories to the USA. The US government used two names for its new lands:

- The 'Northwest Territory' – north of the River Ohio
- The 'Southwest Territory' – south of the River Ohio

The government urged American colonists to set up farms in these lands. This angered the Native Americans. They said Britain had no right to give their lands to the USA. Very soon, bloody **conflicts** broke out between colonists and indigenous peoples.

> ### Reflect
> Look at the map on page 10. Find the following:
> 1 The River Mississippi
> 2 The Northwest Territory
> 3 The Southwest Territory
> 4 The River Ohio

Defeat of the indigenous peoples

President George Washington was worried about the Native Americans of the northwest. He feared that they might help Britain try to win back its thirteen colonies.

Washington spent huge sums of money on a war against the Native Americans. In 1794, the US army defeated them at the Battle of Fallen Timbers in Ohio. A year later, the Native American leaders were forced to accept the Treaty of Greenville. They gave up vast areas of land.

Dispossession of the indigenous peoples

By 1837, the Native American lands had been turned into new states of the USA. (See the red text in the yellow areas on the map on page 10.) Many indigenous people who had once lived there moved further west. They entered land where other Native American tribes already lived. This created conflict between the groups of Native Americans.

4 ▼ Native Americans being forced to accept the Treaty of Greenville. Painted in 1795

> ### Record
> Complete the right-hand column of row 2 in your Tensions Table. Be sure to explain the following:
> 1 Why tensions grew between the Native Americans of the East and white Americans after 1783
> 2 Why the Native Americans resented the Treaty of Greenville
> 3 Why conflicts grew between different Native American tribes.

▲ An 1826 engraving of a settler's small farm and cabin in Ohio. The farmer probably owned about 40 hectares of the forest around the cabin

Land and democracy in the new territories

The United States was one of the world's first democracies. A **democracy** allows its people to have a say in choosing its rulers. In 1801, Thomas Jefferson was President of the USA. He believed that 'yeoman farmers' would make a democracy work well. These were farmers who owned around 100 acres (40 hectares) of land.

Jefferson admired the hard work of farmers and their families. He was sure that farmers would stand up for their rights. They would not let governments grow too powerful.

The cost of getting started

Jefferson encouraged American colonists to move west. He tried to sell all the land very quickly. He divided it into large sections of 640 acres. Each acre cost $1–2. Most farmers barely made $100 a year.

Despite the cost, thousands of white Americans bought some land. They started their own farms. In the far north many became 'squatters'. They settled on the land without paying. They hoped to raise the funds by the time someone came to collect the money.

Reflect

Yeoman farmers faced many challenges. The engraving above shows a farmer's cabin in Ohio. Most of his land is still covered by trees.

Use details in the picture to work out how this colonist family is tackling its challenges.

Land and profit

People called '**land speculators**' made big profits. First, they bought large amounts of land from the government. Then they sold it in smaller plots at a high price to farmers who could not afford to buy 640 acres at a time.

Squatters were furious. They faced a simple choice: pay the new, high price to the speculator or give up and go back east.

> ### Record
> Complete row 3 on your Tensions Table. In the right-hand column, you should mention:
> 1 Why the US government tried to help yeoman farmers
> 2 Challenges faced by the farmers.

Land and trade further west

In 1800, France owned a huge part of North America. They called it Louisiana. (See the purple area on the map on page 10.)

Many feared that the USA and France might fight a war over this area. But, in 1803, Jefferson made a deal with the French. To avoid war, he bought all the French land for just $15 million.

The US wanted to open up trade in this new land. In May 1804, it sent out two explorers, Lewis and Clark. They led a small group up the Missouri River into the Rocky Mountains. Then they went by land to the Pacific coast. (See the map on page 10.)

Contact with Native Americans

Lewis and Clark met many groups of Native Americans on their journey. They usually communicated and cooperated well with the peoples they met. A Shoshone woman called Sacagawea acted as their guide. She helped to build trust. Once, the explorers lost the trust of a chief called Black Buffalo. This almost led to a war.

Lewis and Clark failed to find a river route to the Pacific but their exploration led others to hunt beaver and sell furs to Europe. This and other trades with the Native Americans of the far west grew rapidly. The booming trade, settlement and over-hunting created tensions between indigenous peoples as well as causing ecological damage.

▲ This image from 1939 portrays Lewis, Clark and Sacagawea. It tries to show this as a heroic exploration but the reality for indigenous peoples was very different.

> ### Record
> Complete row 4 of your Tensions Table. In the right-hand column explain:
> 1 How and when the USA gained the French colony of Louisiana
> 2 How Lewis and Clark helped to open up new trade in the West
> 3 How the USA tried to avoid tension with the French and with Native Americans.

> **Record**
>
> Continue your Tensions Table by copying the words in row 5 from page 9.

Exploitation: Cotton plantations and slavery, 1793–1838

This picture shows a group of enslaved people in chains. Slave traders are marching them into Kentucky. They will sell them there.

The years between 1793 and 1838 saw an enormous expansion of **slavery** across the United States.

▲ Enslaved people being taken to Kentucky c.1820, from a book published in 1836. They were being moved to an even more cruel way of working

Divisions over slavery: North and South

By 1789, slavery was being phased out in the seven Northern states of the USA. However, it continued to thrive in the Southern states. It became common to talk about the nation in two halves: 'the North' and 'the South'. Over the years differences grew between the two sides.

Economic differences

The South's great wealth came from **plantations** (farms). These grew crops such as tobacco, rice and cotton. Most of the work on these plantations was done by enslaved black people of African origin.

There were few enslaved people in the North. The land there was not suitable for plantations. Northern businessmen disliked slavery. They said it gave the South an unfair advantage in trade. In the North, employers had to pay their workers. Southern enslavers did not have to do this. It helped them make high profits.

What tensions arose as the USA grew, 1789–1838?

Religious differences

A few Christian groups, mainly in the North, spoke out against slavery. They said that God had made all men to be free.

Other Christian groups in the South preached that God had made black people to serve white people.

Slavery was even dividing people over their Christian faith.

Political differences

The US Constitution said that each state's voting power depended on how many people lived there. Enslaved people could not vote at all but they were part of the state's **population**. This created a problem.

- If enslaved people were counted, their large numbers would give great power to the South. This would anger states in the North.
- If the enslaved people were not counted, the South would be very weak. It might try to become a new, separate country to avoid this.

In the end, the Constitution agreed that enslaved people should count as three-fifths of a person. Many in the North were unhappy.

Reflect

Why might these people be angry that slavery was spreading:

- A Northern businessman
- A Northern preacher
- A Northern politician?

New opportunities for slavery in the new territories

As you learned on page 11, the USA gained new lands from Britain in 1783. America's leaders had to decide whether slavery should be allowed to spread into those new lands.

- Most people in the North wanted the US government to ban all slavery. Some just wanted to restrict slavery to states where it already existed. They hoped it would die.
- In the South, people wanted slavery to be allowed in all new American lands. The Constitution said that the government must not take any person's property. Enslaved people were considered to be property. Southerners argued that this meant the US government could not end slavery anywhere.

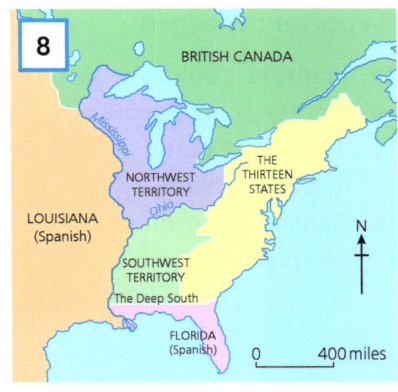

▲ Territories opened by the US government for colonisation by 1790

Slavery spreads in the Deep South

In 1788, the government banned slavery in the Northwest Territory but allowed it to spread to the Southwest Territory.

Straight away, new cotton plantations were opened in the 'Deep South'. These were the lands to the west of Georgia.

Slave traders, like the men shown on page 14, made great profits. They 'bought' enslaved people in old slave states and marched them to the Deep South. They sold the enslaved people to plantation owners there. Traders were often paid over $1000 from the 'sale' of an enslaved person.

The huge profit led some traders to kidnap free black people in the Northern states and to sell them into slavery.

Record

Now complete the second column of row 5 in your Tensions Table. Explain the following:

1. How and why slavery helped to create tensions between the North and the South of the USA
2. How and why slavery spread across the Deep South.

> **Record**
> Continue your Tensions Table by copying the words in row 6 from page 9.

The growth of slavery, 1793–1820

Although Thomas Jefferson was himself a slave holder, he also believed slavery would die out in the long run, but he did not dare to **abolish** (ban) it. He once said that 'we have the wolf by the ears, and we can neither hold him, nor safely let him go'. Three factors helped slavery to grow stronger than ever in the early years of the nineteenth century.

Factor 1: The 'cotton gin'

In the top left of the picture below you can see a cotton plant. Among its white, fluffy fibres are hundreds of tiny seeds. These had to be removed. Until 1793, this was done by hand. Then Eli Whitney invented the machine shown in the picture.

Whitney's '**cotton gin**' (engine) removed seeds from cotton 50 times more quickly than human hands. This brought three important changes:

- Planters could process cotton very quickly.
- Planters could grow a more seed-filled variety of cotton plant.
- This plant could survive in the heat of the Deep South. The less seed-filled variety would have died in that heat.
- Banks expected cotton production to grow. They lent people money to set up new plantations.

Factor 2: The 'pushing system'

After 1793, plantation owners needed their cotton pickers to keep up with the cotton gin. Owners developed what has been called the 'pushing system'. Owners used more enslaved people and forced them to work more quickly. The cotton gin depended on human sweat and toil.

The gin and this new way of working increased the profits of cotton-growing. Slavery was spreading and enslaved people were suffering more than ever.

▼ An engraving showing the value of Eli Whitney's cotton gin, late eighteenth century

> **Reflect**
> In this picture find:
> - a close-up view of a cotton plant
> - enslaved people picking cotton
> - an enslaved person turning the handle to operate the '**cotton gin**'.

What tensions arose as the USA grew, 1789–1838?

Factor 3: The Louisiana Purchase and the 'Cotton Kingdom'

In 1803, the USA purchased the huge French colony of Louisiana (see page 13). Americans quickly moved into that area. They set up three new states in the Deep South. These were Louisiana (1812), Mississippi (1817) and Alabama (1819).

These three states, with Georgia and the two Carolinas, were often called the 'Cotton Kingdom' (see map below).

The port city of New Orleans grew rapidly. Steam boats brought the bales of cotton down the Mississippi River. Sailing ships then took the cotton to the North or to Britain. It was woven into cloth in factories. By 1820, cotton made up 42 per cent of all US exports.

Meanwhile, enslaved people were 'bought' in auction houses in New Orleans. It all helped the Cotton Kingdom to grow.

New Orleans in 1834. This detail from a painting shows steam boats bringing cotton. Behind them, sailing ships are waiting to take it away

Reflect

How did these factors help slavery to spread after 1793:

- The 'cotton gin'
- The 'pushing system'
- The Louisiana Purchase?

The 'Missouri Compromise', 1820

In 1819, leaders in the North and South began a bitter argument. The South wanted to allow all new states to use slavery. The North feared this would give the South too much power. In 1820, the government tried to end the argument by its 'Missouri Compromise'. This said that slavery would only be allowed in the new state of Missouri and in the area south of its border. This deal helped to balance the power of the North and South in the USA. But slavery was still spreading.

The 'Missouri Compromise' of 1820

Record

Complete row 6 in your Tensions Table. Be sure to explain:

1 What the 'Cotton Kingdom' was
2 How slavery grew so quickly after 1793
3 How the 'Missouri Compromise' tried to ease tensions.

> **Record**
>
> Continue your Tensions Table by copying the words in row 7 from page 9.

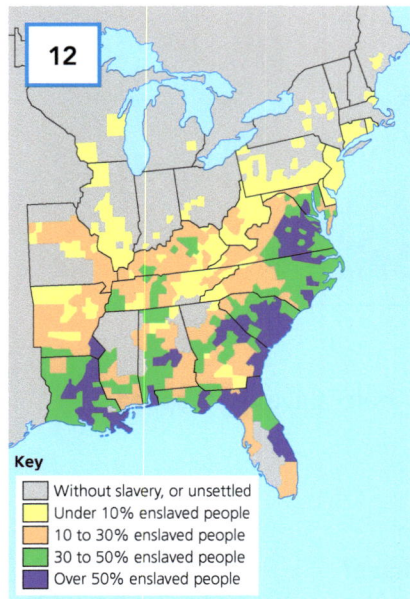

▲ Map showing the number of enslaved people in the USA and where they lived by 1830.

Troubles and tensions grow

Slavery was creating more strains than ever in the USA by 1838.

Strain 1: Growing fears about slavery

In January 1811, some enslaved people rebelled against their captors in the Deep South. It was led by an enslaved man called Charles Deslondes. The freedom fighters killed many white Americans.

The local armed forces ended the revolt in just two days. They cut off Deslondes' hands. He was shot and set on fire. Twenty-five other rebels were killed. Their heads were displayed on sticks.

Some in the North said that well-paid, free workers would not revolt like this. They said the revolt proved that:

- slavery relied on violence from enslavers
- it would cost a lot to keep the South safe from revolts
- the South would be safer if it ended slavery.

But most Northerners shared the South's fear of rebellion. They were afraid of what might happen to the USA if millions of formerly enslaved people won the right to vote.

> **Reflect**
>
> What do you think scared people about the idea of freeing the enslaved people and giving them the vote?

Strain 2: Growing opposition to slavery – the 'abolitionists'

People who worked to abolish (end) slavery were known as '**abolitionists**'. They grew in number between 1800 and 1850. They were not all the same.

- Most abolitionists believed slavery was plainly wrong. It must be ended peacefully.
- Some abolitionists simply disliked the way Southerners tried to tell them what to do. Slave holders in the South told Northern courts that they must send all runaway enslaved people back to their owners. This angered Northerners.
- Some abolitionists wanted to free the enslaved people and then remove them from America. We would now say these were racist views. In 1817, these abolitionists formed a society to send formerly enslaved people to Africa. Almost all enslaved people had lived their whole lives in America.
- Some abolitionists encouraged enslaved people to revolt against the plantation owners. Others were shocked by any calls to violence.

> **Reflect**
>
> Do you think there were tensions between abolitionists?

Strain 3: Growing dependency on slavery

By 1838, few people living anywhere in the USA could say that they were not affected by slavery.

In the South

Only 25 per cent of people in the South enslaved people. Very few owned more than twenty. All enslavers came to depend on their enslaved people.

Even Southerners who did not personally enslave people depended on slavery. These included:

- traders in enslaved people, like those on page 14
- workers on boats that carried cotton and enslaved people
- people who ran the auction houses where enslaved people were sold.

Enslaved families were often broken up. Between 1815 and 1820, 2646 children were sold in New Orleans alone. Their average age was just nine years old.

In the North

People in the North also made money out of slavery.

- Northern factories made cloth from the cotton produced by enslaved people. Factory owners grew rich. Workers had steady jobs.
- Rich people and banks became land speculators. They bought land in the South. They sold it for a great profit. Many of these speculators and land owners never even went to the Deep South. They never saw how enslaved people lived.

More and more people depended on slavery for their wealth. This made it less and less likely that it would simply die away.

Strain 4: Growing power from slavery

Andrew Jackson was President of the USA from 1829 to 1837. He was a Southerner. He openly supported slavery. He allowed banks to lend larger sums than ever to people who wanted to **invest** in any business connected with cotton.

Slavery had powerful supporters. But abolitionists were growing in strength. Slavery was putting the USA under more and more strain. In the end the strain split the nation. You will learn about this in Enquiry 3.

▲ An auction of enslaved people in New Orleans. Buyers used to check legs, arms, teeth and gums. They made some women strip naked to check if they might bear many children, though this was actually impossible to distinguish

Record

Complete row 7 in your Tensions Table. You need to show that slavery affected all of the USA. Explain the following:

1. Why slavery made Americans scared
2. What abolitionists wanted
3. How Americans in the North and South were caught up in slavery
4. How President Jackson encouraged slavery
5. How tensions were growing.

1.3 Expulsion: The forcible removal of indigenous peoples, 1830–38

This map shows the land that became the United States of America. On it you can see the names of some of the Native American tribes that once lived there. By 1800, the US government aimed to treat each tribe fairly as a small, independent nation. By 1838, this approach had been dropped. White Americans and Native Americans were bitterly divided.

> **Record**
> Continue your Tensions Table by copying the words in row 8 from page 9.

▲ Map showing indigenous peoples and nations of North America, c.1829

Indigenous peoples' responses to settlement, 1789–1829

In 1787, the US government allowed white American colonists to move west (see page 11). When they arrived, many of the tribes that lived there moved away. The tribes went further west, out of the reach of the US government and the settlers. In the south-east it was different. The Native American tribes who lived there were already hemmed in by land taken by white settlers.

The Creeks and Seminoles went to war against colonists in the south-east. In 1814, a white American army defeated the Creeks. The Creeks had to give up 23 million acres of land to the white people.

> **Reflect**
> On the map above, find:
> - the Creek tribe
> - the Seminole tribe.

What tensions arose as the USA grew, 1789–1838?

The 'Five Civilised Tribes'

Some white Americans worked to live peacefully with the Creeks. This painting shows Benjamin Hawkins. He was a plantation owner. He learned the language of the Creek Indians. He tried to encourage them to learn from white American culture (way of life).

Another tribe, the Cherokee people tried hard to fit into white culture. In 1825, they built their own capital city, Echota. It was just like Washington. They also created an alphabet so they could write in their Cherokee language. Soon more Cherokee people were able to read than the white people who lived around them. By 1828, they had their own newspaper, the *Cherokee Phoenix*.

The Choctaw, Chickasaw and Seminole nations also opened schools and churches. Together with the Creek and Cherokee nations they became known as the 'Five Civilised Tribes'.

None of this helped to save their homelands.

The Indian Removal Act, 1830

By 1830, Andrew Jackson had become President of the United States. He had led the army that defeated the Creek people in 1814 (see page 20). He did not want the 'civilisation' of Native American tribes. He wanted cotton planters to take over the lands where indigenous peoples lived.

▲ Benjamin Hawkins and Creek people, painted in 1805. He is teaching the Native Americans how to use a plough.

In 1830, Jackson persuaded Congress to pass the Indian Removal Act. This marked out land for Native Americans from the East to live on. The land was referred to as 'Indian Territory'. It was a very long way away. It is shown by purple stripes on the map on page 10.

Thousands of Choctaw, Chickasaw and Creek people felt they had to accept the Act. They began the long journey west across the Mississippi River to the new Indian Territory.

◀ President Andrew Jackson. He did more than anyone to force Native Americans off their lands in the 1830s

Record

Complete row 8 in your Tensions Table. Explain:

1. Why the Native Americans of the south-east did not move west when settlers first took their lands
2. How the 'Five Civilised Tribes' tried to fit in with white culture
3. How and why President Jackson passed the Indian Removal Act in 1830.

Make sure you identify all the tensions involved.

> **Record**
>
> Continue your Tensions Table by copying the words in row 9 from page 9.

Native American resistance, 1830–38

The Cherokee, Seminole and Creek peoples all **resisted** the 1830 Indian Removal Act. The diagram below tells you how they did this. Whatever they tried, they met with no success.

> **Reflect**
>
> Look at the methods of resistance shown in the circle below.
>
> Which of these did the tribes try to use between 1830 and 1838?

The Cherokee Nation and the court

The Cherokee people refused to move from their lands. In 1831 and 1832 they took the state of Georgia to the Supreme Court. They accused Georgia of ignoring their rights as a nation.

The judge agreed that the Cherokees had those rights but he also said that the US government was like a parent – it could decide what was best for the Native Americans.

President Jackson told the state government of Georgia to send more colonists into Cherokee lands.

Seminole wars

Some Seminole people accepted the Indian Removal Act. They were taken to Indian Territory. Other Seminole chiefs went to war to defend their lands. The war lasted from 1835 to 1842. It cost the USA $40–60 million. Some escaped enslaved people joined the Seminole people.

In 1842, the US government invited the Seminole chief to peace talks. It was a trick: they captured him. He died in jail. After this, most Seminole people moved west. In 1858, only about 200 Seminole people were left in Florida. The United States paid them to move west.

Resistance!
- Go to war
- Use small-scale violence
- Go to court
- Get help from others
- Do a deal with your opponents

Creek revenge on white colonists

In March 1832 the Creek Nation gave up most of their Alabama land to white colonists. Each Creek person was promised an individual piece of land in another Creek area. Very few actually got their new land. Land speculators cheated many of the Creek people out of these smaller plots. Some white US citizens simply settled on the plots without permission. The Alabama government did nothing to stop the colonists.

In 1835, some Creek people took revenge. They began stealing livestock and crops from white colonists. Some committed arson and murder. In 1836, the US government ordered the removal of all remaining Creek people. By 1837, approximately 15,000 had moved west.

What tensions arose as the USA grew, 1789–1838?

Cherokee tears – the forced march west

In 1835, a small group of Cherokee people chose to move west to Indian Territory. But most of the Cherokee people refused to move.

In the winter of 1838, the US army forced 18,000 Cherokee people to march to the Indian Territory. Over 4000 of the tribe died of cold, hunger or disease on this thousand-mile march. It has become known as the 'Trail of Tears'.

By 1838, Andrew Jackson's government had forced over 46,000 indigenous people to leave their lands. The 25 million acres of land where they had once lived was given over to white settlement and to slavery.

▲ *The 'Trail of Tears'*, painted by Robert Lindneux in 1942

Reflect

How has the artist captured the mood of the 'Trail of Tears' in this painting?

Record

Complete row 9 in your Tensions Table. In the right-hand column explain how the Cherokee, Seminole and Creek peoples tried to resist the 1830 Indian Removal Act. Mention:

1 the Supreme Court
2 wars
3 attempts to do deals
4 the 'Trail of Tears' in 1838.

Review

An education company has asked you to help create a revision app. It is for students studying the growth of the USA, 1789–1838. It will use a touch-screen map of the USA. Touching part of the map plays an audio track. It explains when and how the USA expanded in that area.

1 Choose just one row from your Tensions Table. Use it to write an audio script. It must give a clear and organised summary of those events. It should:
   a) say when, how and why the USA expanded into that area
   b) explain what tensions that expansion reveals.
2 Draw a simple map of the USA and shade the area that you have written about. This is to show which part of the screen would trigger the audio.

CLOSER LOOK 1

Slavery: Hands, fingers and blood

In 2014, the American historian Edward E. Baptist published his book *The Half Has Never Been Told*. It tells the stories of enslaved people. He organised each chapter around a different part of the human body. A chapter called 'Blood' explains how enslaved families were often split up. This meant that blood relations never saw each other again. Another shows how enslaved people became 'hands' that worked for their enslavers.

This 'Closer look' introduces you to one of the enslaved people in Baptist's book. The chapter's title is 'Fingers'. You will learn why below.

Fingers: A new type of slavery

Charles Ball grew up on a plantation in Maryland. At that time he worked under the 'task system'. This set each enslaved people a number of tasks to do each day. When these tasks were done, they had time to themselves.

This all changed by 1805 when Ball was sold to work in Georgia in the Deep South.

The 'Pushing System'

Eli Whitney's cotton gin put pressure on enslaved people. It could clean raw cotton quicker than they could pick it. Plantation owners found a way to make the enslaved people keep up with the gin. This was the 'pushing system'.

- The fastest pickers worked at the head of a line of enslaved people.
- This worker set the pace for the rest.
- The overseer pushed the first pickers to work really hard.
- The others had to keep up.

Ball and other enslaved people who were being forced to pick cotton worked from before dawn until after sundown. They made their fingers work faster and faster.

On his first day, Ball picked seventeen kilograms of cotton. This set his minimum. If he ever picked less than this he was brutally punished. The photograph shows what whipping could do.

Between 1805 and 1860, the amount of cotton picked in the Deep South increased sixfold. The only 'machines' that did this were the fingers of the enslaved pickers.

Work, resistance and punishment

The enslaved pickers did find ways to resist. Some dared to work slowly or broke tools. Others hid rocks in the cotton to add weight. In 1828, a black preacher, Nat Turner, even raised an army of freedom fighters. They killed 60 white citizens. Turner was captured and he and others were brutally killed.

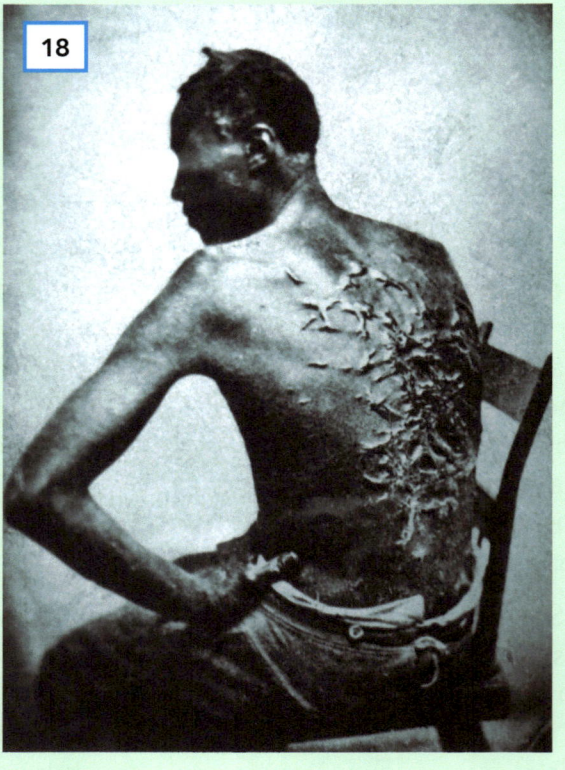

▲ An enslaved man from a Louisiana cotton plantation who had been whipped by his owner, Captain John Lyon. Photographed c.1860

KEY IDEA 1

Causes – why slavery grew, 1789–1838

Charles Ball's life was shaped by events he could not control. When he was born around 1780, slavery had more or less died out in the North. Many thought the same would happen in the South. Instead, it spread more quickly than ever before. It also became crueller than it had been. Charles was caught up in that change.

Cotton plantations and slavery spread rapidly between 1789 and 1838. Here are some factors that made this happen:

Investment:
Banks in the North and in Europe helped slavery to spread. They invested in (put money into) new cotton plantations to get them started. In return they took a share of the profits.

War:
When the USA defeated Britain in the war of 1776–83, it won the right to take new land west of the Appalachians. Without new land, slavery could not spread.

Demand:
'Demand' means that customers want to buy something. By the 1820s, there was great demand for cotton. Mill owners in Britain and the North wanted as much cotton as they could get from the South. They wove it into cloth and sold it for a profit.

Government:
In 1788, the US government officially allowed slavery to spread in the new lands in the South.

In 1803, the US government bought the French colony of Louisiana. It allowed slavery to spread in the southern part of this huge area.

19

This part of the Louisiana Purchase to be free of slavery

SPANISH TERRITORY

Key
---- Limit of British ruled colonies, 1776
Area where slavery was allowed, 1839

0 400 miles

Communications:
By the 1820s, powerful steamboats and early **railroads** appeared in the South. These:
- cut the time and cost of sending raw cotton to customers
- speeded up the movement of enslaved people to plantations in the Deep South.

Technology:
From 1793, Eli Whitney's cotton gin meant:
- more cotton could be cleaned more quickly – so more land was needed to grow it
- tougher, seed-filled cotton plants could be grown. These could survive the extreme heat of the Deep South so plantations could spread there.

2 Visions

How did different groups see the American West, 1839–60?

▲ *Storm: Waiting for the Caravan*, by Alfred Jacob Miller, 1858

There is a vast mass of land between the Mississippi River and the west coast of America. White Americans called this area 'the West'. It has many different features, including:

- huge plains of grasslands
- mighty rivers
- baking deserts
- towering mountains
- deep ravines.

The mountain men

In the 1820s, white fur trappers (many from the US, but also from around Europe) crossed **the Plains**. They moved up into the Rocky Mountains. They were known as 'mountain men'. They hoped to make a fortune by trapping animals for their valuable fur.

During the 1830s, hundreds of mountain men met each year in the Rocky Mountains. They would buy and sell furs. They also traded rifles, traps, knives, coffee and whisky. These were brought in each year by a long caravan (trail) of wagons from the East. This painting shows the caravan in the Rocky Mountains in a rainstorm.

The Native Americans

As you can see in the painting, Native Americans guided the caravan through the mountains. As many as 2000 Native Americans would attend the mountain men's gathering. They traded fur and buffalo hides for guns, knives and whisky. They also were eager to trade for metal pots, kettles and jewellery.

How did different groups see the American West, 1839–60?

Moving west

From 1840, this changed. That early friendship of mountain men and Native Americans was lost.

- Trading posts replaced the great yearly meeting.
- The army arrived. It built forts to protect trade.
- Large groups of white migrants arrived. Each had its own **vision** of what this new land offered.

▲ Moving west

After 1840, these new groups of migrants wanted the land of the West. White Americans and Native Americans had very different ideas about how to live there. These differences would eventually lead to conflict and war.

The Enquiry

In this Enquiry you will learn about the lives of four groups of people. Each group had its own vision of how to live in the West in the period 1839–60.

1. **The Plains tribes** who lived on the vast grasslands of the American West.
2. **The early migrants** who travelled over the Plains and the Rocky Mountains to begin new lives in Oregon and California.
3. **The Mormons** who built a city in the desert at Salt Lake.
4. **The gold miners** who hoped to make a fortune by digging for gold in the Rocky Mountains after 1849.

Different things mattered to each of these groups. You will make an A3-size summary chart about each one. We will offer advice and support.

Each chart will look different. Here is an outline of what your first chart will look like.

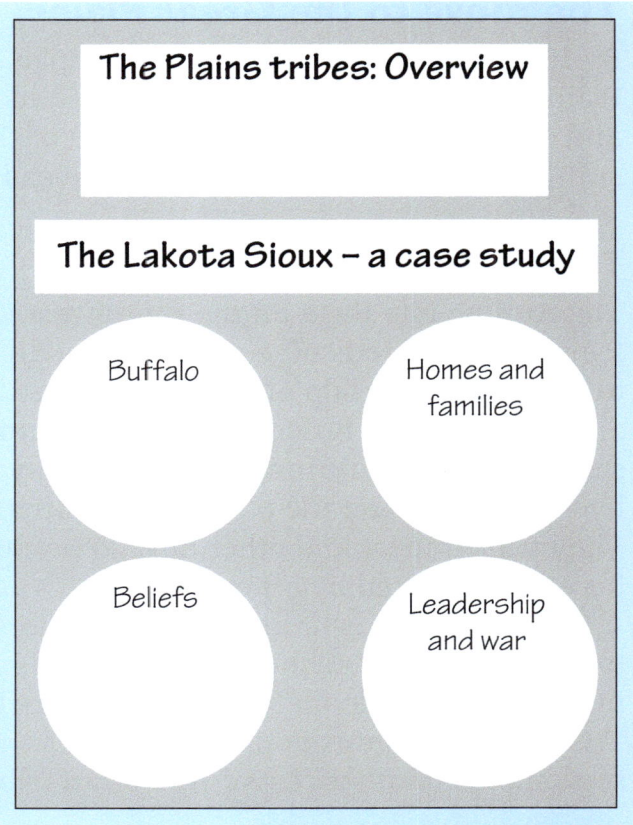

2.1 The Plains tribes

At first, white Americans saw the Great Plains as a desert. It had few trees and little water. Huge herds of buffalo grazed on the vast grasslands. Several Native American tribes lived by hunting the buffalo.

In 1837, the artist Alfred Jacob Miller made a sketch of a buffalo hunt. He later turned this into the oil painting you see here.

▲ *A Surround* by Alfred Jacob Miller, 1858

The move to the Great Plains

By 1840, a number of indigenous peoples lived on the Great Plains (see map on page 27). Each had its own history and culture. But they shared a vision of the land and were similar in some ways. Here are three examples:

Reflect

What impression do you get from Miller's painting of:
- the nature of Great Plains?
- the skills of the Native Americans who lived there?

The Apache

The Apache had lived on the south-west Plains for hundreds of years. They used to hunt single buffalo on foot with bows and arrows. They hunted in the spring and summer. In the autumn and winter, they lived in villages on the edge of the Plains. They traded meat and other buffalo products for corn produced by other tribes.

Then Europeans brought guns and horses to America. The Apache started to hunt huge numbers of buffalo on horseback with rifles. They also used guns and horses to raid the settlements of other Native American tribes. They stole their corn and stopped trading. Apache warriors were feared across the south-west Plains.

The Cheyenne

In the eighteenth century, the Cheyenne lived on the edge of the northern Plains. They survived by farming and hunting. They hunted on horseback, killing buffalo with guns.

Buffalo had always been an important source of food for the Cheyenne. They now used buffalo as a trade item as well.

How did different groups see the American West, 1839–60?

By the 1830s, the Cheyenne had become **nomads** like the Apache. This means they had no fixed home. They moved from place to place hunting on the Plains.

They still traded. They exchanged guns and horses with the Apache. They supplied buffalo meat and skins to the new white trading posts. In return they received guns, powder and alcohol.

The Cheyenne sometimes fought fierce horseback wars on the Plains. They did this to keep control of hunting grounds.

The Lakota Sioux

Before the 1830s, the Lakota Sioux lived on the northern edge of the Plains near the Great Lakes. They had once hunted buffalo on foot each summer. They also grew small amounts of crops to help them survive the winter.

From the 1780s, other Native American tribes were moving into Lakota Sioux homelands. They were escaping the expansion of the United States.

The Lakota moved their whole tribe to the Plains. They gave up farming. Instead they became nomads. They followed the buffalo herds. By then, horses and guns were more easily available as white traders moved west. This helped the Lakota Sioux to hunt buffalo on a larger scale. At the centre of this new life were the Black Hills of Dakota. These became a symbol of Lakota power.

> **Record**
>
> Start your first summary chart. Use the model on page 27.
>
> Copy the top box. Then add your own notes to show what the Apache, Cheyenne and Lakota Sioux had in common.

4 ▲ A detail from *Sioux Buffalo Dance* by George Catlin, c.1832

The Lakota Sioux – a case study

This section (pages 29–31) provides a case study of one of the three Sioux tribes that lived on the northern Plains – the Lakota Sioux.

1 Hunting the buffalo

The Lakota used buffalo for food, clothing and shelter. Buffalo blood could provide liquid when no water was to be found.

Before a hunt, the Lakota would perform a 'Buffalo Dance'. The hunters dressed as buffalo and danced around in a large circle. They called to the spirit world for a successful hunt.

A few buffalo hunts per year could provide a small Lakota band with enough food to survive. However, the Lakota often killed many more buffalo than necessary. On one hunt a group killed 1400 buffalo but kept only the tongues. These were a great delicacy. The rest of the animals' bodies, including the meat, were left to rot on the Plains.

2 Homes and families

Lakota families lived in **tipis**, large tents made from buffalo hides. These were stretched over wooden poles. They were perfect for nomadic life.

- They could be put up or down very quickly.
- They would not be blown over by the wind.
- The flaps at the top let out the smoke from the fire inside.
- In summer, the hides at the bottom of the tipi could be rolled up to let air inside.

The men hunted, fought and looked after the horses. Women prepared food, made items from buffalo and put up or took down the tipi.

The Lakota valued children highly. Parents and relatives prepared them for adult life.

Old people were respected for their wisdom. But when they became too old and weak to keep up with the band, they were often left to die. The survival of the band was more important than the life of an individual.

5 ▲ A view of a Lakota Sioux camp by George Catlin, c.1830s

Record

Use what you have learned so far to add notes in your Plains tribes summary chart. Write them in your 'Buffalo' and 'Homes and families' circles (see page 27).

Reflect

Why do you think we asked you to make your notes about the Lakota in circles?

3 Beliefs

Like many Plains tribes, the Lakota believed in the Great Spirit. All living things, including rocks, streams and trees, had their own spirit. Circles were important to the Lakota. The circle of the horizon surrounded them. The sun and moon shone above them. The seasons returned like a circle year after year. Lakota life showed the power of circles. Settlements, meetings, dances and tipis all took a circular form. Many Lakota still share these beliefs today.

How did different groups see the American West, 1839–60?

The Lakota believed that all living things came from the land. No one could own land. By the 1800s, they said it was wrong to dig the earth and grow crops. He Sapa (or the Black Hills of Dakota) was sacred land for them. Many Lakota were buried there.

4 Leadership

The Lakota people were made up of a number of tribes. Each tribe had many bands. There were between 10 and 50 families in a band. Bands and tribes chose their own leaders. A full tribe met to make only big decisions about war or trade. There was no single leader of all the tribes. The US government made treaties with the Lakota. Some tribes would follow the treaties. Others would ignore them.

5 Warfare

The Lakota were fierce rivals with other tribes. They fought to steal horses and control hunting lands. Warriors on foot were no match for the horse-riding Lakota. By 1839, the Lakota were the strongest tribe on the Plains.

Men joined warrior societies (rather like teams). They stole horses or fought bravely in battle to bring honour to their society.

Each society had its own customs, songs, costumes and dances. Women could not usually join the societies. But there were a few great women warriors, such as Buffalo Calf Robe and Moving Robe.

> ### Record
>
> Now add the final notes to your Plains tribes summary chart.
>
> 1 Write your notes in the 'Beliefs' and 'Leadership and war' circles.
> 2 You can add some simple images to your summary chart. Choose ones that will help you to remember key points about how the Lakota Sioux lived on the Plains.

6 ▼ *A Sioux War Council* by George Catlin, 1847

2.2 Migrants to the Far West

> **Record**
>
> Your next summary chart is about the migrants who moved to the Far West. Set it out in three columns like this.
>
> | Migrants to the Far West | | |
> |---|---|---|
> | Reasons for moving | Challenges faced | Impact on Native Americans |
> | | | |
>
> This page will help you to complete your 'Reasons for moving' column.

In the early 1840s, people from the East started to move to the Far West of America. By 1860, around 443,000 had moved to the West Coast territories of Oregon and California.

Why migrants moved

Several factors led migrants to move to the Far West:

Factor 1: From 1837–46, the economy of the USA faced real problems. People lost savings and jobs. Many wanted a fresh start in the Far West.

Factor 2: Advertisements, like the one here, told people life was better in the Far West. They promised good land and a fine climate. Early colonists sent encouraging reports back east.

Factor 3: In 1841, the US government passed a law to help farmers in Oregon. It said that anyone who built a house there would be first in line to buy the land around it. This helped to block land speculators.

Factor 4: In 1845, journalists and politicians in the East began to write about 'Manifest Destiny'. This was the idea that God had a plan for white Americans to settle the whole of North America. He wanted them to convert the Native Americans to Christianity.

Factor 5: By 1840, mountain men and explorers had mapped the routes and trails which would allow settlers to make the 2000-mile journey to the West more safely.

> **Reflect**
>
> How does the advertisement make the Far West seem like a good place to live?

▲ An advertisement for Singer sewing machines, 1881

How did different groups see the American West, 1839–60?

Making the journey

The colonists' journey to the Far West was nearly 2400 miles long. It took around eight months to complete. Americans, Norwegians, Swedes, Germans, Irish and Canadians all went. Over 3000 black Americans had migrated to California by 1850. They all wanted to start a new life there.

The journey to the Far West was long and difficult. Early colonists were often guided by mountain men and Native Americans. They still needed stamina, courage and good luck. Many trusted God to give them strength.

Boxes 1–4 in this chart lead you through the migrants' journey.

> ### Record
> This page will help you to add notes in your 'Challenges faced' column.
>
> You can use sub-headings like these:
> - Weather
> - Disease
> - Enemies
> - Finding help

1 Migrants often spent the winter in one of the towns on the Missouri River. They built their wagons there. They also stocked up flour, bacon, salt, coffee and sugar. In spring, they set off on their long trek to the Far West. Most travelled in 'trains' of twenty or more wagons for safety.

2 The migrants followed the Platte River across the Great Plains. Their wagons covered less than 18 miles a day. They had to deal with baking sun, torrential rain, rivers, buffalo and hostile Plains tribes. They would stop at Fort Laramie or Fort Kearny for rest and supplies.

4 At Fort Hall some migrants took the route south to California. Others went north to Oregon. Migrants to California had to cross a desert and the Sierra Nevada mountains. The Oregon migrants often struggled to cross the Blue Mountains. Native Americans in canoes paddled some of them down the rivers. Others left their wagons and continued the journey on foot.

3 Next they had to cross the Rocky Mountains. This was the hardest part. They struggled through the mountain passes with wagons, baggage and animals. There were frequent accidents. Many died of diseases such as cholera (serious diarrhoea). If autumn snow trapped them in the mountains, they might starve to death.

> ### Reflect
> Prepare a short role play with a partner. It is 1845. You live in the east of the USA. One of you is keen to move to the Far West. One of you is not. One must give reasons for going west. The other must explain why it may be dangerous and difficult. Use your notes to help you.

Case study: The Sagers on the Oregon Trail

▲ The Whitman Christian Mission, Oregon, 1840s

The Sager family

Henry Sager began the move to Oregon in May 1844. He went with his six children and his heavily pregnant wife, Naomi. They travelled with a group of 323 other emigrants.

Henry's daughter, Catherine, kept notes about their journey. She recorded details such as the following:

- The family's wagon overturned as they crossed the Platte River.
- Catherine broke her leg when she jumped from a moving wagon, like one in the image above. She was dragged under the wheel. Her leg never fully recovered.
- Disease struck the group at Fort Laramie. Henry Sager died. He was buried but other travellers later dug up the grave. They were searching for any goods buried with him.
- Naomi became ill soon after Henry's death. She lay crying out to her dead husband. She too died. The Sager children became orphans.

The Whitman Mission

In October, the Sager children reached a Christian Mission in Oregon. It was run by Marcus and Narcissa Whitman. They were trying to convert the local Native Americans. Narcissa adopted the Sager children.

In 1847, measles swept through the area. It killed many Native Americans. They blamed the Whitmans for these deaths. They murdered Marcus and Narcissa. They set fire to the Mission. Only Catherine and three of her sisters survived. Eventually Catherine married and settled down in Oregon.

Catherine Sager's remarkable account can be misleading. Far more migrants died from disease than from attacks by the indigenous people. Many Native Americans helped settlers. They made money by providing ferry travel, food and supplies.

> ### Reflect
> Compare the experiences of the Sager family with the notes you have already made in your 'Challenges faced' column.

The impact of the colonisation of the Far West on Native Americans

In the 1840s, some of the Native Americans formed positive relationships with migrants. The trails to the Far West crossed their lands. They would:

- act as guides
- help migrants to cross rivers
- supply migrants with food in return for goods from the East.

Tensions on the Plains

More and more migrants came. The different visions of the West started to cause tension.

The government wanted to gain full and speedy access to western lands. In one speech, **Senator** Douglas of Illinois asked:

> How are we to develop and protect our immense possessions on the Pacific (coast) with a vast wilderness, filled with hostile savages cutting off all direct communication? The Indian barrier must be removed. 10

Reflect

Senator Douglas describes the Great Plains as a 'vast wilderness'. Why would the Native Americans disagree with him?

In 1851, at Fort Laramie, tribes such as the Lakota Sioux, Northern Cheyenne, Arapaho and Crow made a treaty with the US government. They said the white people could establish forts and safe routes across the Plains. In return, they wanted something to make up for the damage this would do to their hunting. In 1853, Southern tribes made similar agreements with the US government.

The Lakota were granted greater hunting rights on the south side of the trails west. Smaller tribes such as the Crow were outraged that the Lakota Sioux got better treatment than they had. This led to splits between the Native American tribes.

Conflict in Oregon

In 1855, the US government signed a treaty with the Yakima tribes of Oregon Territory. The Yakima gave up huge areas of land to the USA for settlement. The treaty said that no white people would move in for two years. But colonists rushed onto the land within twelve days of the treaty being signed.

The Yakima felt cheated by the US government. They began raiding white settlements. The US army was called in. A priest of a Spanish Christian Mission agreed to protect some Yakima. The army burned the Mission to the ground.

By 1858, the Yakima had lost 90 per cent of their lands. Twenty-four of their chiefs had been hanged or shot. White Americans and the Native Americans of the Far West were in clear conflict.

Reflect

From what you have read, do you think it is fair to say the US government broke its treaties with the Native American tribes?

Record

1. Add notes to the third column on your 'Migrants to the Far West' summary chart. Be sure to mention:
   - how some Native Americans helped migrants at first
   - how the Native Americans' hunting lands became the cause of conflict
   - why treaties about land did not work.
2. Underneath your chart, draw some suitable images to help you recall key points.

2.3 The Mormons

> **Record**
> You will find instructions and hints for your third summary chart on page 37.

The **Mormons** are a religious group. Their first leader was Joseph Smith. He claimed that God had shown him a secret, golden book. In 1830, Smith published this as *The Book of Mormon*. It said that Jesus had come to America after he rose from the dead.

Smith believed he must rebuild the church in America. It must be exactly as *The Book of Mormon* described it. The members of this church became known as Mormons.

Mormons believed that all land and property should be shared. This made them popular with poor Americans. Many were converted. But the Mormons were not popular with other Americans:

- Some objected to the Mormon vision of land ownership.
- Some disliked Joseph Smith. They said he ruled his Mormon people like a king.
- Many objected to the way Mormons were very keen to convert people.
- Very many were shocked that Mormons practised polygamy. This allowed men to have more than one wife. The aim was to increase their numbers more rapidly.

Mormon visions of the West

The Mormons were so unpopular that they were forced to move from New York and then Ohio in the 1830s. They still wanted to set up their own 'holy city' and live by their Mormon beliefs. So, in 1838, they started a town in Illinois. It was called Nauvoo.

Once again local people turned against the Mormons. In 1844, Joseph Smith tried to become President of the USA. Soon afterwards he was shot by a mob.

Brigham Young (c.1855) had 55 wives

> **Reflect**
> Why do you think the mob killed Joseph Smith?

The new Mormon leader was Brigham Young. He had read there were large, unsettled lands in the region called Utah. They were near the Great Salt Lake. In spring 1846, Young led a great column of Mormon emigrants out onto the Plains. They were moving west again.

The journey to the Great Salt Lake of Utah

The Mormons travelled on foot with their belongings in handcarts. After nearly 1300 miles, they arrived at the Great Salt Lake (home to the Shoshone, Ute and Paiute). Here, in 1847, the Mormons founded Salt Lake City. By 1852, over 10,000 Mormons were living there.

The Mormon settlement of Utah

Brigham Young kept tight control over the settlement at Salt Lake. He said no one had the right to own land. The church would grant land. Each family would get what it needed. The Mormons believed Young was close to God. They would follow his orders.

Salt Lake was a very dry place. It was hard to grow food. Young told people to dig water channels. These brought water from distant mountain streams to the Mormons' farms. Everyone had a fair share of the water.

In 1850, a US government surveyor described the city in glowing terms:

> Through the city itself flows an unfailing stream of pure, sweet water ... spreading life and beauty over what was a barren waste. **12**

But like elsewhere, colonisation led to conflict and suffering for indigenous people.

Reflect
Do you think it was helpful that Young had so much power over his people?

13

▲ Salt Lake City, 1853

Growth and conflict in Utah

Utah was added to the USA as a territory in 1850. Brigham Young was its first governor. From 1850 to 1860, Mormon towns spread rapidly over Utah. People in the East feared the Mormon religion was spreading. They decided to act.

Because Utah was not a state, it could not make its own laws about property ownership or marriage. In 1857, the government made plans to bring Utah in line with US laws. In September 1857, a band of Mormons led by John D. Lee killed 120 migrants who were travelling to California. Lee blamed the Paiute, but it was quickly proven that the Mormons had played the key role. Lee believed they were US army spies. The scandal forced Young to step down as governor. Utah was then made to follow the laws of the rest of the USA.

Record
Make your own version of this summary chart. There are some hints in each section.

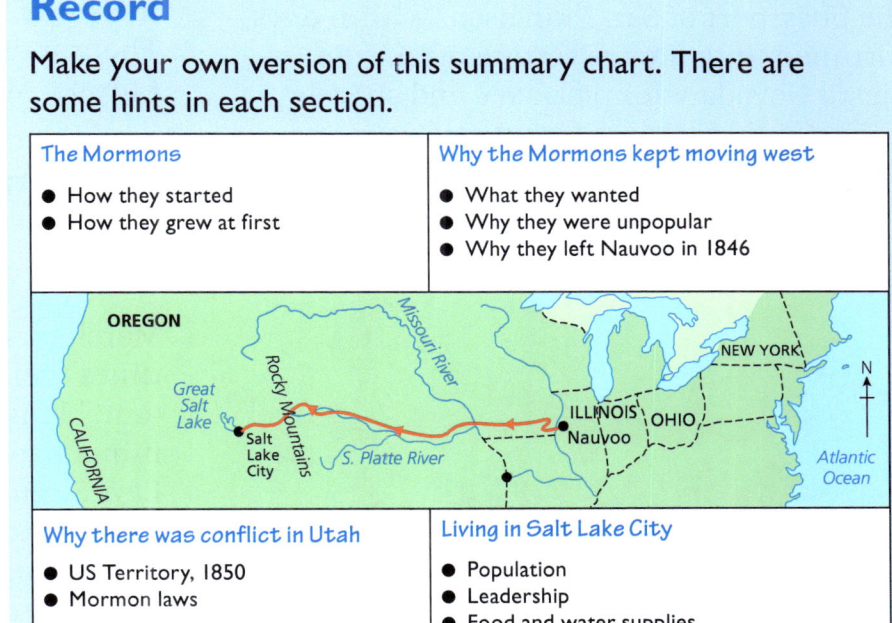

The Mormons	Why the Mormons kept moving west
● How they started ● How they grew at first	● What they wanted ● Why they were unpopular ● Why they left Nauvoo in 1846

Why there was conflict in Utah	Living in Salt Lake City
● US Territory, 1850 ● Mormon laws	● Population ● Leadership ● Food and water supplies

2.4 Gold miners

> **Record**
>
> Your final summary chart will be about two 'gold rushes'. It must help to show similarities and differences between the two. In particular it must show:
>
> - when and how the gold rush started
> - how news of finding gold was spread
> - how many went in search of gold
> - where they came from
> - how they travelled to the gold fields
> - how the gold rush helped others earn
> - how the gold rush affected the area
> - how the gold rush affected Indians.

In January 1848, a worker at a timber mill in California had a stroke of luck. He found gold in the foothills of the Sierra Nevada mountains. By May, this news had reached the busy port of San Francisco. Within days, fortune-hunters were setting off for the Sierra Nevada with pick-axes and shovels.

These first miners found gold in rivers and streams. It had been washed out from the huge deposits buried deep in the mountains. Soon, diggers were opening small mines to reach the underground gold.

The California gold rush, 1848–49

In early 1848, wild stories spread about the gold in California. It was said that:

- miners were making $1000 a day (the average US wage was $2–3 a day)
- men were washing $16 or more of gold dust from their beards each night.

At the end of 1848, the US president announced that there really was gold in California. This led to a wild frenzy. In 1849, over 50,000 migrants rushed to the gold fields.

- Some dared to sail from the East around the tip of South America.
- Most used the California Trail to make their way west on foot or by wagon.
- Thousands of the gold diggers came from Europe, Mexico and China.

Making money without striking gold

Some made profits without digging for gold:

- Merchants sold supplies for five to ten times their normal prices. A pan, pick, tent, blanket and food could set a new miner back $100.
- Levi Strauss sold hardwearing denim trousers to the miners.
- Nancy Gooch was a freed slave. She was a cook for some miners. She earned enough to buy the freedom of her son and his wife back in Missouri.

14 ▲ Miners panning for gold in California

> **Reflect**
>
> What equipment are these miners (left) using?

The impact of the California gold rush

The miners who rushed to California hoped it would make them rich. For almost all of them it had a different impact. By 1852, mining had become big business. Companies employed hundreds of men. Miners who had once hoped to get rich quick ended up working for these companies. They received tiny wages. They had to dig out and move tons of rock. Big machines crushed the rock and washed it with chemicals. This released the gold.

The California gold rush changed the West for ever. Here are some of the ways it did this:

▲ San Francisco, c.1850. In early 1848, the population of San Francisco was about 500. By the end of 1849 it was 25,000

Impact on California's wealth and influence

- California had enough people to become a US state in 1850.
- Mining towns grew up in the mountains.
- San Francisco became a major city with a thriving sea port.
- Lumbering and farming spread quickly to supply mining towns with wood and food.
- Demands for a railroad link to the East grew.

Impact on the land

- In the 1850s, high-powered water jets were used to blast rock from the mountains. Whole hillsides were eaten away by the process.
- Waste gravel clogged the rivers.
- Floods washed away whole towns.
- Chemicals killed fish and wildlife.

Impact on the Native Americans

- As their lands suffered, tribes struggled to survive.
- In 1848, some Native Americans began to dig for gold. Other miners drove them into the mountains or shot them dead.
- In the 1850s, a new California law said that Native Americans without a job could be sold for slave labour. Hundreds were sold to white colonists.

Record

Complete the part of your chart about the California gold rush. Remember to cover all the points shown on page 38.

The Pike's Peak gold rush, 1858–59

> **Record**
>
> Start the second part of your summary chart. Follow the advice given on page 38.

The next major gold rush came in Kansas Territory. This included the area which is now Colorado. In the 1850s, gold hunters moved into the area known as Pike's Peak.

In July 1858, gold was finally discovered. By the end of the month, the news had reached the East. Gold fever broke out again. A trade slump in the East made people even more keen to go west. More than 100,000 people made the journey to Kansas by 1859.

There were differences between the way miners reached Pike's Peak and the way they reached California.

▼ A sail wagon, from an 1860 magazine. This was a real invention for crossing the Plains

16

Transport links

- New railroads helped people travel from the East to St Joseph with ease.
- From there it was just 600 miles to the Pike's Peak gold fields.
- The Plains were easier to cross than the mountains that guarded the Far West.
- As the image on this page shows, some people even tried to use sail wagons to speed across the Plains.

> **Reflect**
>
> Why was it easier for people to reach Pike's Peak than California?

'Town boosters'

- Men called '**town boosters**' published maps that lied about the routes. The men claimed the best route to the gold fields was through their town.
- One map of the central route showed the Smoky Hill River reaching the gold fields. In fact, it stopped well short.
- One group on the central route ran out of water and food. A man ate a fellow traveller and half of his own brother before an Arapaho (Native American) helped him back to a town.

> **Reflect**
>
> The map on page 41 shows 'Starvation Trail' (near Smoky Hill River). Why do you think it has been given that name?

How did different groups see the American West, 1839–60?

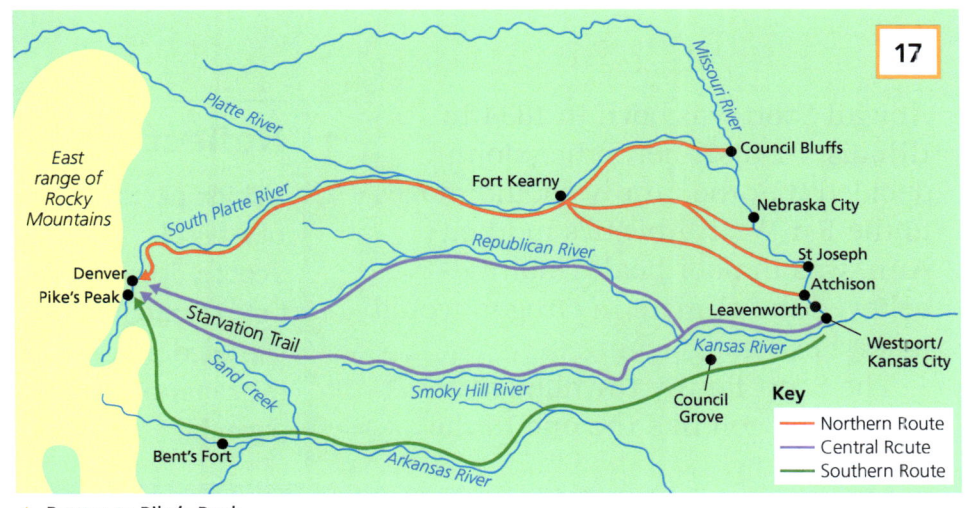

▲ Routes to Pike's Peak

> **Reflect**
>
> On this map find:
> - Kansas City (in the East)
> - Pike's Peak (in the west)
> - the Rocky Mountains.

The impact of Pike's Peak

As in California, traders and others made money when gold was discovered at Pike's Peak. There were two more very important consequences of gold mining at Pike's Peak:

Impact on the centre of the USA

- Mining towns in west Kansas needed food. Families started farms in the eastern area to supply them.
- The population of the eastern half of Kansas grew quickly. It became a state in 1861.
- After Kansas became a state many more people began to settle there. St Joseph became a hub for settling on the lands in the centre of the USA.
- Mass **migration** to the West had begun.

Impact on Native Americans

- Earlier treaties allowed white people to cross Native American lands (see page 35). But now the white people wanted to settle on the Plains.
- White farmers allowed animals to graze on Cheyenne and Arapaho hunting lands.
- White miners moved into areas where the Cheyenne and Arapaho spent the winter.
- In talks with Native Americans the US government showed its point of view. It expected the Native Americans to give up their vision of the West and allow the white vision to succeed.

In September 1859, a Kiowa man rode into a shop in a white settlement in Colorado. He spat blood in the shopkeeper's face. It was a sign of more blood to come.

Record

Finish your summary chart. Now highlight in different colours:

- how the gold rushes were similar
- how the gold rushes were different.

Review

1. Look at your four summary charts. Choose the two groups that you think had the most contrasting visions of life in the American West.
2. Explain why those two groups saw the American West so differently.

CLOSER LOOK 2

The diary of Abigail Scott

Abigail Scott was born in 1834 in Illinois. In 1852, her father, John, decided that the family should move to the Far West. Abigail's mother, Ann, was in poor health. John believed the climate in Oregon would make her strong again.

The Scott family travelled in a covered wagon like the one in the picture below.

Abigail Scott kept a diary. Here are some extracts about her journey west.

Reflect
Which parts of Abigail Scott's diary below match the account of migrants on page 33?

12 May 1852: Passed a place, where some folks were burying the remains of a young man who had died with the measles. The family had lost three of their company in St. Joe … They have become entirely discouraged. They were about to go back home.

20 June 1852: Our mother was taken about two o'clock this morning with a violent diarrhoea and cramps. She did not wake any of us until daylight. By then there was nothing we could do to save her life … She now rests in peace.

18 June 1852: We started early and passed Fort Laramie about 10 o'clock. We passed several Indian trading posts this morning … The tribe of Indians that occupy this territory are called Sioux. Some say they are thievish but it is thought if emigrants are careful they need fear nothing from them.

28 August 1852: Two months and seven days after our beloved mother died and the ruthless monster death … [has] taken in his icy grip the treasure of our hearts! Last night our darling Willie was called from earth, to be with angels around the throne of God … He was four years of age … He often before his illness talked of dying and wanted to die and meet his mother.

▲ *Approaching Chimney Rock*, a painting by W. F. Jackson, 1865

KEY IDEA 2

The consequences of migration

Abigail Scott was just one person. But hundreds of thousands of migrants moved west between 1839 and 1860. The overall consequences of this were enormous. For centuries, Native Americans had lived on the Plains, in the mountains and in the land between those mountains and the sea. In just two decades, those lands and the lives of the people who lived there changed forever.

Here is a reminder of some of the main points you learned about in Enquiry 2.

The top briefly summarises what mattered most to each of the three main migrant groups. These were their 'visions' of the West.

The lower half of the diagram shows some of the consequences of these people moving west.

Migrants from the East and from Europe **wanted to start new lives** in the Far West. Many wanted to farm land that they believed was 'wasted' by Native Americans.

Mormons moved west to escape persecution in eastern cities. They **wanted to build a new, 'Holy City'** where they could live freely according to their beliefs.

Miners moved into the mountains of California (1849) and Colorado (1858). They **wanted to 'get rich quick'**. Most ended up working for big, industrial mining companies.

Thousands of migrants started **farms in California and Oregon**. Treaties failed to protect tribes like the Yakima who lost 90 per cent of their land.

The large **ports** of San Francisco and Portland opened America to new trade in the Pacific. This helped the USA grow richer.

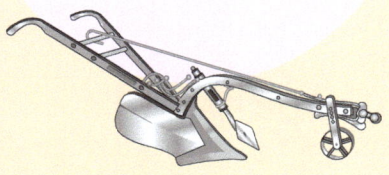

24

By the Treaty of Laramie (1851), the US paid Plains Indians money for allowing migrants to cross their lands. Towns and army forts grew up along the routes. This all **disturbed buffalo hunting lands**. Tribes fought about who could hunt where.

Near Salt Lake City, **tribes lost access to water** supplies that they had always used.

Land and water supplies were polluted in the gold fields.

White settlers started the first **farms and towns on the Plains** near Colorado. These provided food and goods for miners in the mountains nearby.

43

3 'A new birth of freedom'?
What sense can be made of the Civil War and its aftermath, 1861–77?

In a civil war, a nation is split. Its people fight against each other. The American Civil War was fought between the North and the South. It lasted from April 1861 to April 1865. It took the lives of over 750,000 soldiers and civilians.

The Fort Pillow Massacre

The painting below shows a terrible event in the war. It took place at Fort Pillow in Tennessee. Three hundred Northern soldiers held the fort. Almost all were black formerly enslaved people. In 1864, a large force of Southern soldiers surrounded them. The soldiers raised a white flag. They walked out of the fort. Their surrender was ignored. The soldiers of the South killed many of them in cold blood. Historians think some women and possibly children were killed too.

In 1863, President Abraham Lincoln had declared that the war could be 'a new birth of freedom' for the United States. Clearly this 'new birth' came at a terrible cost.

> ### Reflect
> In the image find the following:
> 1 Southern soldiers (in grey)
> 2 Northern soldiers (in blue)
> 3 Women and children
> 4 An army general directing the battle.

1

▼ *The Battle of Fort Pillow*, painted in 1885

What sense can be made of the Civil War and its aftermath, 1861–77?

The great divide between 'North' and 'South'

This map shows how the United States was divided during the Civil War.

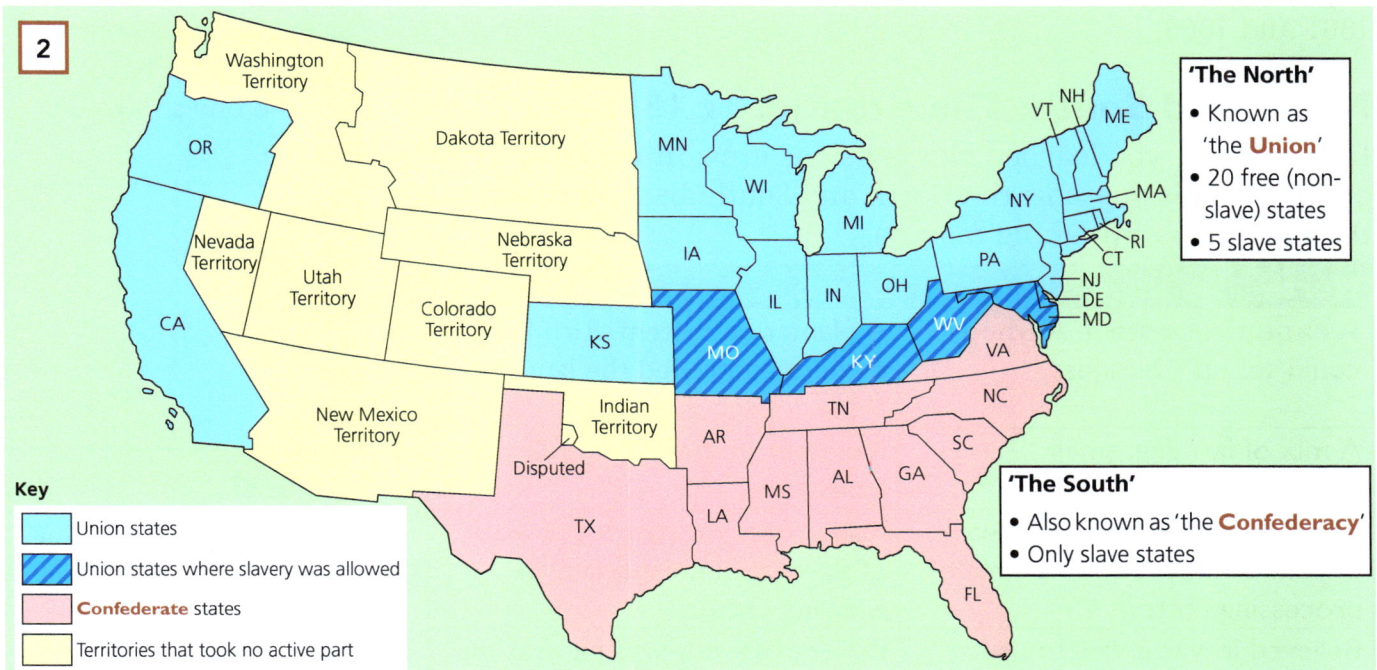

The Enquiry

People like to sum up big historical events in short, simple sentences. This often leads to over-simplified statements.

Your challenge in this Enquiry is to correct some over-simple summaries about:

1. Divisions over slavery and the causes of the Civil War
2. The African-American experience of the war, 1861–65
3. The years of **Reconstruction** after the war.

You will gather notes in three summary tables. Your first summary table will start like this:

Divisions over slavery and the causes of the Civil War	
'Slavery divided the North and the South and caused the Civil War'	
The statement is partly right because …	The statement should be adapted because …

45

3.1 Divisions over slavery and the causes of the Civil War

As pages 46–49 will show, there is no simple, single explanation for the conflict that tore the USA apart between 1861 and 1865.

North and South: The situation, c.1850

In Enquiry 1, you learned how tensions grew in the USA. This chart reminds you how the North and South disagreed about their economies (making money).

North	South
A **capitalist** system. Anybody could set up a business.	A plantation system. Rich land owners controlled the land and trade.
A mix of farming, small businesses and factories.	Mostly large plantations. Little industry.
Made money through the work of paid employees, for example processing cotton.	Made money through the work of slave labour, especially in growing cotton.
Believed it was unfair to use enslaved people as workers. It helped the South grow rich as enslaved people were not paid for their work.	Believed slavery was natural and right. Believed the North treated its factory workers badly. It called them 'wage-slaves'.

Despite their differences, both North and South depended on slavery.

- The North needed cotton from the South. Many Northerners worked in factories that made cotton cloth.
- The South needed money from the North. It was invested in the cotton plantations.

Banks in the North, in Britain and all around the world helped to set up new plantations. They did this for a share of the profits. By 1850, the cotton produced in the USA was worth $1.3 billion ($578 billion today). These profits went to people in the North and the South. The people who made no money were the 3.2 million enslaved black workers who grew, picked and cleaned the cotton.

> **Record**
>
> Start your first summary table. Copy the headings from the one shown on page 45.

> **Record**
>
> The chart (left) will show you how slavery did help to divide the North and the South.
>
> Use the chart to add notes to the left column of your summary table.

> **Record**
>
> Now add notes in the right column of your summary table. You must show how the North and the South both relied on work done by enslaved people.

What sense can be made of the Civil War and its aftermath, 1861–77?

Abolitionists

People who tried to end slavery were called 'abolitionists'. By 1850 there were many of these in the North. Here are some reasons why the number had grown:

- In 1831, William Lloyd Garrison founded *The Liberator*. This newspaper spread abolitionist views.
- In 1833, Garrison helped to start the National Anti-Slavery Society. It had 250,000 members by 1838.
- Formerly enslaved people who had escaped their captors told their stories. The most remarkable was Frederick Douglass (right). He even toured Europe to win support.
- Abolitionists like Harriet Tubman (another escaped enslaved person) set up the 'Underground Railroad'. This smuggled escaped enslaved people to freedom in the North. It won a lot of support.
- In 1851, Harriet Beecher Stowe published *Uncle Tom's Cabin*. This novel laid bare the horrors of slavery. It sold 2 million copies in ten years.

▲ Frederick Douglass, c.1850

All these abolitionists lived in the North. Their ideas became more popular there. The South grew angry.

> **Reflect**
>
> Which of the abolitionists above do you think did most to upset Southern slave holders?

Threats to the power of the South

From 1846 to 1850 Congress argued about whether slavery should be allowed or banned in California. This was in land taken from Mexico. If slavery were not allowed there, the South feared it would not be allowed anywhere in the West.

In 1850, a pro-slavery Southern politician, Henry Clay, persuaded Congress to reach a compromise. This gave the South hope that slavery might extend westwards. Here is what 'Clay's Compromise' said:

- California should be a free (non-slave) state but …
- … other territories gained from Mexico should be allowed to decide for themselves if they wanted slavery.
- A new Fugitive Slave Act should be passed to make all states return people who escaped slavery to their captors.

> **Record**
>
> 1. In the left column of your table, add notes about how abolitionists turned the North against slavery.
> 2. Add notes about 'Clay's Compromise'.
>   a) Does it show that disputes over slavery were still very deep?
>   b) Or does it show that the disputes did not have to lead to war?

> **Record**
>
> Continue your summary table. In your left column you should mention:
> - divisions caused by the Kansas–Nebraska Act
> - divisions between the Democratic and Republican Parties.

North and South: The struggle deepens, 1850–60

In 1854, Congress passed a law that pleased the South. This was the Kansas–Nebraska Act. In 1820, the Missouri Compromise had banned slavery in these two territories (see page 17). But this new 1854 Act allowed them to vote on whether or not they wanted slavery. This alarmed the North and all abolitionists.

Abolitionists and slave holders wanted their side to win the vote. Both sent supporters into Kansas and Nebraska. In the next few years, there was some shocking violence between them.

Democrats and Republicans

- The South relied on the **Democratic Party** in Congress.
- Democrats wanted more power for state governments and less for national government.
- After 1854, many Northern voters thought the Democrats were too keen to please the South.
- After 1854, most support for the Democratic Party came from the South.

- Nearly all support for the **Republican Party** came from the North.
- It was set up in 1854 by people who objected to the Kansas–Nebraska Act (see above).
- It said slave holders had too much power.
- It won support from business owners, shopkeepers and small-scale farmers.
- It also got support from abolitionists.

President James Buchanan

A Democrat called James Buchanan became President in 1856. He wanted to spread slavery north of the Missouri Compromise line (see page 17). This would mean the land would be filled by large plantations. This upset Democrats in the North. They wanted small farms to be started in those new territories. In the presidential election of 1860 they switched their vote to the Republican candidate. He was called Abraham Lincoln.

'Honest Abe' Lincoln

Abraham Lincoln liked to be called 'Honest Abe'. He did not like wealthy slave holders. He admired Americans who worked hard. This campaign poster tried to impress them. It shows how he used to split logs into fencing rails when he was young.

Lincoln promised to give free land to Western colonists. He also promised to stop the spread of slavery. He said it was dividing the United States.

▼ A Republican poster showing Abraham Lincoln as a 'rail splitter', 1860

What sense can be made of the Civil War and its aftermath, 1861–77?

States' rights and the descent into Civil War, 1860–61

Lincoln won the election in November 1860. Leaders in the South were sure he would end slavery. They saw this as an attack on 'states' rights'. They believed each state had the right to decide its own way of life. They said the South would 'secede' (break away) from the USA to defend this right.

The start of the Confederacy

The South quickly took action to start its own new nation:

1. The state of South Carolina voted 169 to 0 to secede from (leave) the Union. It did this just days after Lincoln's victory.
2. During the winter of 1860–61, six more states left the Union. They joined South Carolina to form the 'Confederacy'.
3. In February 1861, the Confederacy elected its government. It was led by the slave holder, Jefferson Davis. He said the Confederacy was standing up for the rights of states. If they voted to break away, the President could not stop them.

The first shots are fired

Lincoln took up his role as president on 4 March 1861. He said it was illegal for the South to leave the USA. He insisted that all army forts in the South were still the property of the US government. He was testing the South. Would it take the forts by force? If so, it would be the South that started the war.

On 12 April 1861, Confederate soldiers opened fire on Union soldiers in Fort Sumter. This guarded Charleston harbour in South Carolina. On 15 April, Lincoln gave his orders to his generals. The army must force the Confederacy to come back into the United States. The USA was at war with itself.

▼ The Confederate bombardment of Fort Sumter. From an engraving made in 1861

> **Reflect**
>
> In the 1860 election, did Lincoln say he would abolish (end) slavery? (See the bottom of page 48.)

> **Record**
>
> Add notes to the right column of your summary table. Start like this:
>
> *'After Lincoln won the 1860 election, the South started the Confederacy. Its leaders said they did this because ...'*

> **Record**
>
> By now you should have your own ideas about what caused the Civil War. Write your own simple summary. You could start like this:
>
> *'There is no doubt that slavery divided the North and South by 1860. The real question is whether it caused the war. I think it did/did not [choose one] because ...'*

3.2 The African-American experience of the war, 1861–65

For African Americans, the Civil War had two phases. We start by learning about the first two years of the conflict.

Phase 1: 'Limited war', 1861–62

When the war started in 1861, slavery continued in the South and in the North. It even continued in the 'border states'. These were the ones that had decided to fight with the North on the side of the Union.

Life for most black Americans carried on as it had done before the war. Here are some of the main features:

> **Record**
>
> Start your second summary table. Copy the headings shown on page 51.
>
> In the left column, use examples from the diagram below to show how life carried on for African Americans in the North and in the South.

African Americans in the North (Union) …			
Jobs	**Housing**	**Education**	**Society**
Did not get equal access to jobs. A few educated black men did get good jobs.	Most lived in poorer parts of cities. They had worse houses than white people but paid more rent.	Black children went to different schools from white children. There were a few black universities.	Public places **segregated** (split) black people from white people. There was lots of racism from white people.

Key
- Union states
- Border states
- Confederate states
- Territories

African Americans in the South (Confederacy) …			
Jobs	**Housing**	**Education**	**Society**
Almost all black people were enslaved. They had no money.	Most enslaved people lived in small cabins. Few comforts. Disease was common.	In most of the South, the law said black people must not learn to read or write.	Enslaved people were property not people. They must not share public places with white people.

50

What sense can be made of the Civil War and its aftermath, 1861–77?

'Contrabands'

In 1861, free black men living in the North rushed to join the Union army. But they were not allowed to. Lincoln feared the border states might decide to fight for the South if he let black men join the Union army.

In the South, a few enslaved people did work for the Confederate army. They were not allowed to fight. They just built defences or moved supplies.

As Union forces pushed into the South, large numbers of enslaved people fled the plantations. Many ended up working for the Union army. But they were still not allowed to fight. These freedom seekers became 'contraband of war'. This meant they were captured property. They did not have to be sent back to their captors. They could work for the Union army, though not as soldiers.

▲ Union troops and contrabands in the Civil War, c.1864

First signs of freedom

In July 1862 Congress passed a new law. It said that when the Union army took any slave-holding land, the enslaved people there became free.

On the Sea Islands off the coast of South Carolina there were 10,000 enslaved people. Union troops captured the islands in 1861. In 1862, they were freed. They could keep the land to farm for themselves.

Northern volunteers (mainly women) soon came to help the Sea Islanders. They offered healthcare and education. Among them was the black abolitionist heroine, Harriet Tubman. Tubman had spent decades helping people escape slavery in the South; now she came to the Sea Islands to be a nurse.

Reflect

How did life change for:
- 'contrabands'
- enslaved people living on the Sea Islands?

▼ Harriet Tubman, c.1893

Record

Here are the headings for your second summary table:

The African-American experience of the war	
'During the Civil War, the daily lives of black Americans carried on much as before'	
Reasons to agree	Reasons to disagree

Phase 2: 'Total war', 1863–65

> **Record**
>
> Continue your summary table.

On 1 January 1863, Lincoln made his historic **Emancipation Proclamation**. This said that all enslaved people would be freed as soon as the Union won the Civil War. Limited war was over. Slavery would now either triumph or die. This was 'total war'.

Black regiments from South and North

Black Americans could now join the Union army.

- In autumn 1862, the first black regiment of formerly enslaved people was formed in South Carolina.
- In January 1863, the first Northern black regiment was set up. Many more followed.

By the end of the war, 70 per cent of Northern black men (33,000) joined the Union army. They played a major role in later victories.

White people worked and fought alongside them. This helped many to see black Americans as real people. But black soldiers were not always treated well.

- They could not become officers.
- They often did the hardest, lowest jobs.
- They were paid less than white soldiers.

A few black soldiers were executed for demanding equal pay. Some white soldiers refused to be paid until wages were equal. In June 1864, equal pay was granted. But black soldiers still could not be officers.

▼ Black soldiers' duties in the Union army. From the *Frank Leslie Newspaper*, 1865

> **Reflect**
>
> This image shows black soldiers doing many different army jobs.
>
> Which of the jobs do you think they would never have done as enslaved people?

Opportunities for people who had been freed from slavery in the South

It was not just men who joined the Union army in 1862. Harriet Tubman served as a scout and a spy. Susie King Taylor, who had been freed from slavery, served as a battlefield nurse. She even taught poor white soldiers to read and write.

The US government also tried to help people who had been freed from slavery:

- It sent teachers and by 1865, 200,000 people who had been freed from slavery had learned to read and write.
- From 1863, the North ran cotton plantations on lands taken in the South. These employed thousands of people who had been freed from slavery. Whipping was banned but wages were very low. They were not allowed to leave the plantations.
- In the final months of the war, General Sherman freed thousands of enslaved people in the South. He was allowed to give each one 40 acres of land and a mule. The land was taken from slave holders' plantations.

Some people who had been freed from slavery did not take government support. They found paid jobs such as labourers, firemen or barbers. Some started businesses and earned over $45 a month.

A disturbing sign in the North

In 1863, Congress passed a new law. It said all men aged between 20 and 45 must join the army. Rich men could avoid being called up by paying $300. Poorer white men felt that they were being forced to fight for the freedom of black Americans.

In July, the white working classes of New York went on a four-day rampage. It was a disturbing sign of problems ahead.

- They attacked places that employed black workers.
- They burned down the houses of black families.
- Worst of all, they **lynched**, drowned or beat many black citizens to death.

Record

1. Complete your summary table.
2. Write your own simple summary about how much daily life changed for African Americans during the Civil War.

▲ Newly free black Americans learning to read, c.1870

Reflect

1. Which type of government support would have felt most different to a person who had been freed from slavery?
2. Which type of support do you think would have helped them most?

▲ An engraving of a lynching in the New York riots, 1863

3.3 Reconstruction and betrayal, 1865–67

The Confederacy surrendered just before 4 p.m. on 9 April 1865. By this point, nearly 750,000 Americans lay dead. Now the destruction was over. The next challenge became known as 'Reconstruction': the rebuilding of the nation.

> ### Record
> Here are the headings for your third summary table:
>
> | Reconstruction and betrayal, 1865–77 ||
> |---|---|
> | 'The Reconstruction years from 1865 to 1877 were a betrayal of African-American hopes' ||
> | Reasons to agree | Reasons to disagree |
> | | |

Presidential Reconstruction, 1865

Lincoln had started to reconstruct the USA before the end of the war. On 31 January 1865, Congress passed the Thirteenth **Amendment to the US Constitution**.

> **13th Amendment to the Constitution of the USA**
> Neither slavery nor involuntary servitude shall exist within the United States.

In a speech near the end of the war, Lincoln made a promise to the South. He said he would work to rebuild the country 'with malice toward none [and] with charity for all'. It was a fine promise. But we will never know if he could have made it work.

▲ Abraham Lincoln

Assassination

Just days after the South surrendered, Lincoln was killed. As he watched a play with his wife, he was shot in the brain. The murderer was John Wilkes Booth. He hated Lincoln for freeing black Americans.

Millions attended Lincoln's funeral procession. As they mourned, no one knew if Reconstruction could still take place.

> ### Record
> 1 In the right-hand column of your table, explain how the Thirteenth Amendment built up African-American hopes.
> 2 In the left-hand column, explain how Lincoln's death betrayed African-American hopes.

President Johnson's Reconstruction u-turn

It was the vice-president, Andrew Johnson, who took over as president when Lincoln was murdered. Many abolitionists believed that he would continue to make black Americans more equal. But he let them down. His main aim was not to treat the South too harshly.

13

▲ Engraving of Andrew Johnson, 1865

Johnson's early aims	Johnson's early actions
To bring the country back together after the war.	Allowed the Confederate states to rejoin the USA straight away. They kept all their pre-war powers.
To punish the South's war leaders.	Planned to punish the South's very top generals.
Not to punish others in the South.	Planned to pardon 16,000 other soldiers.
To avoid forcing states to pass laws they did not want.	Allowed Southern states to govern themselves with little interference.
To protect poor white people in the South from the North's big business power.	Gave land back to white people that had been handed to formerly enslaved people.

The situation by December 1865

In December 1865, President Johnson said Reconstruction was finished. But enormous problems remained.

Some rich plantation owners would not swear loyalty to the Union. Despite this, Johnson allowed them to take control of their state governments in the South.

These new state governments did not dare to bring back slavery. But they passed laws that had much the same effect. These laws became known as the '**Black Codes**'. They were not the same in every state but they all limited the rights of black people. Here are some of them:

Examples from the 'Black Codes'

Black people …
- cannot serve on juries
- cannot give evidence against white people in trials
- cannot marry white people
- cannot own guns
- cannot rent or own farmland.

Reflect

1. Would any of these early actions of President Johnson please black Americans?
2. Why do you think Johnson chose not to treat the South harshly?

Record

Most of your notes from this page will be in the left column of your summary table. Mention the following:

- President Johnson's early actions
- New state governments in the South
- The 'Black Codes' in the South:
  - What they were
  - What they said
  - How they affected black Americans.

> **Reflect**
> 1 Who were the 'radicals'?
> 2 Look at the events shown in the chart below. Which do you think would have most pleased people who had been freed from slavery?

Radical Reconstruction, 1866–70

Many Republicans in Congress were angry. President Johnson was a Democrat who had agreed to work with the Republicans. But he was not handling Reconstruction very well. The most upset were the **radicals**. This group of Republicans wanted to get to the roots of problems. They said the Southern states:

- had lost the right to rule themselves by starting the Civil War
- should be run by Congress until they showed they could be trusted
- should be occupied by the Union army so that it could protect black rights.

These radicals worked to undo Johnson's changes. They got Congress to put a new Reconstruction plan into action.

February 1866

Congress set up a Freedman's Bureau. The government still had some land that had belonged to slave holders. It gave it to formerly enslaved people. But it had very little land to share out. It also helped formerly enslaved people with health and education.

March 1866

Congress passed a law to stop any states from taking away the **civil rights** of some of its people. President Johnson thought this was interfering in state government but he had to accept the new law.

June 1866

Congress passed the 14th Amendment to the Constitution. It said that anyone of any race was a full citizen of the USA if they were born there.

November 1866

Republicans did very well in elections to Congress. This allowed them to be even more radical.

January 1867

Black men in Washington DC were given the right to vote.

March–July 1867

Congress passed three Reconstruction Acts. These:

- took away the powers of Southern state governments
- put the US army in charge of the South
- banned anyone from voting if they had fought for the South in the Civil War
- told the army to protect all black people's rights
- ordered all Southern states to give black Americans the vote. They could only have their own state government again after they did this.

> **The 14th Amendment to the Constitution of the USA**   14
>
> All persons born or naturalised in the United States, and subject to the jurisdiction thereof, are citizens of the United States and the State wherein their reside. No State shall make or enforce any law which shall abridge the privileges or immunities of citizens in the United States; nor shall any State deprive any person of life, liberty, or property, without due process of law; nor deny to any person within its jurisdiction the equal protection of the laws.

Over the next year, the work of Reconstruction went ahead in the Southern states. The army generals were now in charge there.

The radicals' achievements continue

The radicals had more success in the next few years.

- By June 1868, seven Southern states had met the standards set and were re-admitted to the Union. The three remaining states were not far behind.
- By the 1870s, over 2000 black Americans were elected to political posts. These ranged from the **Senate** down to state governments (see the image below).
- In July 1868, the 14th Amendment became law. It was a landmark change. It said that all black Americans could be full citizens of the United States.

More signs of hope for the radicals

Soon the radical Republicans had more good news. In the election of November 1868, Andrew Johnson was voted out of office. The new president was an ex-Union army general, Ulysses S. Grant. The radicals liked the way he had stood up to Johnson and had spoken out on behalf of black Americans.

In February 1869, the Fifteenth Amendment to the Constitution was accepted. This said that male US citizens of all races had the right to vote. At this point, the radicals must have felt that everything was going their way. It did not last.

▼ Part of a display showing photographs of members of the State Government of South Carolina, 1876

The 15th Amendment to the Constitution of the USA

The right of citizens of the United States to vote shall not be denied or abridged by the United States or by any State on account of race, color, or previous condition of servitude.

Record

This time you will mainly be making notes in the right column of your summary table. The hopes of black Americans were being met in the years 1866–68. You need to mention:

- the radicals
- some of the main achievements from page 56 and above
- amendments to the Constitution that protected civil rights
- the growing number of black politicians in state governments.

> **Record**
>
> Continue your summary table. Your notes for pages 58–59 will mainly go into the left column.

Reconstruction loses its way, 1870–77

The pace and direction of Reconstruction fell away after 1870.

Southern resistance

Many Southerners were angry that the US government was interfering in state affairs. They also resisted radical ideas.

- They mocked people in the South who shared the radicals' views. They called them 'Scallawags'.
- They hated 'Carpetbaggers' who came from the North to buy and sell ex-plantation land. (They were named after the luggage they carried.)
- They feared that illiterate black people would ruin the South for ever.
- They accused the North of using bribery and corruption to control the South.
- They believed the South was being driven into debt to pay for Reconstruction.

The claim that black voters were ruining the South was unfair. A person had to own a certain amount of property before he could vote. Most black citizens were too poor to qualify.

Corruption in politics certainly did occur. But this happened all over the USA.

Debts were run up to fund Reconstruction. But without some significant borrowing like this, the South could never be rebuilt.

Southern leaders spread their complaints and fears. Many white voters listened to them. The South was fighting back.

Radical weaknesses and black American fears

▲ Engraving of sharecroppers in the Deep South, c.1875

The radical Republicans did badly in the 1874 elections. Many of their best leaders had died. In 1872, the Freedmen's Bureau shut down. It was short of funds.

Meanwhile, in the South, violent racist groups were on the rise. Members of the Ku Klux Klan wore sinister white robes. They bullied or even murdered black voters. The White League was similar, but less secretive.

All voting was done in public. If a black farmer voted for a radical, he might lose his land, his home or his life. Many black families were '**sharecroppers**'. They paid rent by giving two-thirds of their crops each year to a white land owner. The land owner could evict them if they voted for radicals.

From 1875, President Grant did far less to help the black citizens. Many white voters said he had done enough for black people already. Even Northern newspapers suggested that black Americans should by now be able to stand on their own feet.

Supreme Court rulings

In the 1870s, the Supreme Court hurt the hopes of black Americans.

1. In 1873, it decided that there was nothing in the Constitution to say that state governments must treat all people equally. States in the South could now have separate parks, schools, and restaurants for black and white people.
2. In 1875, it ruled that the US government had no power to protect black voters in the states. Black people gave up on voting. White voters soon elected ex-Confederate officers to run the Southern states.

Left to fend for themselves

By the mid-1870s, Americans were interested in opening the West. They did not care so much about the old struggles of the Civil War. In 1877, the government withdrew the soldiers who had been sent to protect the formerly enslaved people in the South. Black citizens were left to fend for themselves.

A cartoonist created the image below in 1874. He shows black Americans living under threat from the White League and the Ku Klux Klan. As the text in the centre of the image says, this life was 'worse than slavery'. They felt betrayed.

> **Reflect**
>
> Look at the two Supreme Court rulings above. Which one do you think would most upset black Americans?

> **Reflect**
>
> The cartoonist has tried to show how black Americans in the South lived in fear by 1874. How has he done this?
>
> Look closely for details to help you, for example what has happened to the school house?

> **Record**
>
> Use your table to help you write your own simple summary about whether black Americans were betrayed during the Reconstruction years.
>
> **Hint:** Do not forget to mention the years when Reconstruction was going well for black Americans.

▲ A cartoonist's view of the life of black Americans in the South of the USA by 1874

CLOSER LOOK 3

John Brown: Fanatical abolitionist

Most Northern abolitionists used peaceful methods to argue their case. John Brown was different.

Brown felt God was calling him to stop slavery spreading and end it forever. He thought he must be an angel of death. He should use violence to do God's will.

'Bleeding Kansas'

In 1854, the territory of Kansas was thrown open for settlement. There was going to be a vote there about whether Kansas should become a slave state (see page 48).

Pro- and anti-slavery colonists rushed in. There was brutal violence between supporters of each cause. This gave the new territory the nickname of 'Bleeding Kansas'.

Bloody revenge

In 1856, Brown learned that pro-slavery colonists in Kansas had attacked an anti-slavery town called Lawrence. Brown made his way to Kansas. Some of his own sons lived there. Together they kidnapped five pro-slavery colonists. They hacked them to death with swords.

Brown's actions fed further violence. More than 200 lives were lost in Kansas in just three years.

▲ A portrait of the abolitionist, John Brown, 1859

The attack on Harper's Ferry

Three years after his Kansas butchery, Brown wanted to start a full-scale rebellion against slavery. He decided to steal US army weapons and ammunition. These were held in an arms store at Harper's Ferry.

Brown planned to use the arms to attack slave plantations. He would free the enslaved people and arm them. He hoped his army of free men would bring slavery to an end.

The attack went ahead on 16 October 1859. It was a dismal failure.

Brown was taken prisoner. The portrait above shows him wrapped in his prison cloak. He defended himself passionately at his trial. He was still found guilty. On 2 December 1859, he was hanged. Some in the North saw him as a hero and martyr in the abolitionist cause.

Reflect

Look back at the sections on 'abolitionists' on pages 18 and 47. Which abolitionist was most likely to approve of John Brown's violent methods?

KEY IDEA 3

Change – and how to describe it

John Brown was dead before America's enslaved people were set free in 1863. If he had lived to see that day, he might have believed that God's will had been done. But things change over time.

Historians often try to make their own judgements about change. They do this by:

- identifying important changes and
- 'weighing them' against each other as in the diagram below.

The diagram below identifies key changes that affected people who had been freed from slavery during the time known as 'Reconstruction' (1865–71).

The judgement in this case is about whether the changes were positive or negative.

> **Reflect**
>
> Which way do you think the see-saw would tip? When you make up your mind about this, do not just count how many changes are on each end of the see-saw. You must think about which ones were most important.

Positive changes for black Americans

31 Jan 1865: The 13th Amendment to the Constitution banned slavery from the USA.

Jan 1866 to December 1874: Radical Republicans dominated Congress.
They passed:

- the 14th Amendment that said no state could pass laws that would make some people second-class citizens

- the 15th Amendment that said no ex-slave should be denied the right to vote. Some African Americans found good jobs and were well-educated. Some were elected to state governments.

Negative changes for black Americans

Autumn 1865: 'Black Codes' started in the South. These laws limited the right of formerly enslaved people, for example to own land, serve on juries or give evidence against white people in trials.

1873: The Supreme Court said it was lawful to segregate (keep apart) black people from white people, for example in parks or restaurants.

1875: The Supreme Court said the **federal** (US) government could do nothing to enforce the Fifteenth Amendment.

After Jan 1875: Democrats dominated the new Congress. It stopped helping formerly enslaved people. Few black people in state governments were re-elected.

4

Smoke and blood
Settlement and conflict on the Plains, 1861–77

In 1845, the writer John O'Sullivan wrote an article in *The Morning Post* newspaper. He introduced Americans to the phrase 'Manifest Destiny'. This was the idea that God had given North America to the United States. God's plan was for white Americans to spread progress, freedom and democracy across the whole of America.

O'Sullivan did not mention slavery. Nor did he mention the indigenous peoples. They, of course, lived on the land that he thought white Americans should occupy.

A picture of 'Manifest Destiny'

White American artists tried to portray the idea of 'Manifest Destiny'. The picture below was painted by Frances Palmer in 1868. This was exactly when white Americans had begun to settle in the middle of America on the Great Plains.

Reflect

In the painting, find these signs of 'Manifest Destiny':

- Land waiting to be taken by white colonists
- A church with its small belltower
- A school
- A proud couple standing in the doorway of their new home
- Hard-working colonists
- Wagons heading further west

Settlement and conflict on the Plains, 1861–77

Frances Palmer's painting is an imagined scene. It is based on what really happened on the Plains in the 1860s and 1870s.

Between 1861 and 1869 a great railroad was built. It connected the eastern and western halves of the United States. This was a turning point for the American West.

- From the 1860s, cattle **ranchers** began to raise cattle on the Plains.
- White Americans built homesteads and began to farm there.

> **Reflect**
>
> Look closely at the train in the painting on page 62. How can we tell that it is crossing the USA from New York to San Francisco?

The impact on Native Americans

On the right of Frances Palmer's painting are two Native Americans on horseback. They are choking in the smoke from the train. This may be a symbol of how the indigenous peoples of the Great Plains suffered as white people took over the Plains.

In the 1860s and 1870s, the Plains became a battleground. Native American chiefs led their people against the US army.

> **The Enquiry**
>
> In this Enquiry you will find out about the people who transformed the Plains in the years after 1861. They were railway builders, ranchers and **homesteaders**. You will also study the conflict between US forces and the Native Americans in the period between 1861–77. Your challenge is to plan three clear and detailed explanations. These must answer the following questions:
>
> 1 How did the railroads and ranches change the Plains?
> 2 How did homesteaders survive and thrive on the Plains?
> 3 Why was there so much bloodshed on the Plains between 1861 and 1877?
>
> As you read each section, you will prepare several small cards. Each card will record clear, accurate information.
>
> You will use the cards to plan answers to the questions shown above.
>
> **Keep all your cards safely!** You will be able to use them to plan all sorts of answers to all sorts of questions.

> **Record**
>
> Here is a simple practice task. It should help you understand how to make your own cards later in this Enquiry.
>
> Copy these cards. They could help you answer a question about 'Manifest Destiny'. Add extra details if you like.
>
> | Manifest Destiny – God's plan for white colonists in North America | Manifest Destiny's view of progress:
• Take land
• Build schools
• Work hard |
> |---|---|
> | 'Manifest Destiny' was first used in an 1845 newspaper article | Manifest Destiny said nothing about:
• Slavery
• Native Americans |

4.1 How did railroads and ranches change the Plains?

Record
As you read pages 64–65, make a set of cards about railroads. Page 65 gives you some hints.

▲ A photograph taken on 10 May 1869. It shows the scene as the Central Pacific and Union Pacific Railroads met at Promontory Point, Utah

On 10 May 1869, a great crowd gathered at Promontory Point in the Utah desert. They were there to watch as the final spike was hammered into a vital section of railway. In fact, the man given the honour of doing this job missed the spike with his silver hammer. That did not matter. A telegraph operator sent the message that America was now connected from coast to coast. America now had a '**transcontinental**' railroad (railway). In New York and San Francisco cannon were fired. Politicians made speeches celebrating this great achievement of the United States.

Reflect
How can you tell something special is happening in the photograph above?

Building the railroads
President Lincoln had been keen to have a railway like this. He said it would:

- help businesses
- help migrants to travel to the Far West
- allow people to set up farms in the West.

In July 1862, Lincoln approved the Pacific Railroad Act. This offered US government money to railroad companies. To get the money they had to link the east and west of the USA. The Act also offered the railroad companies large areas of land on either side of the track. They could sell this land to settlers. The Act said Native Americans lost any rights over this land.

Money and land

By 1864 the government had built up funds of $50 million. Work could start. The government gave the railroad companies over 6000 acres of land for every mile of track they built across the Plains. One company started building the track from the West. Another started from the East.

The impact of the railways on the Plains

Thousands of workers arrived to build the track; 12,000 came from China. They did the dangerous work of tunnelling through mountains.

On the Plains, men worked six days a week. They worked in baking sun and winter snow. They lived in tents. Accident and illness took many lives.

After the line opened in 1869, a network of track spread across the West. These railroads had a great impact:

Impact 1: On the Plains, towns emerged. They helped the cattle trade. They saw much drinking, gambling and violence.

Impact 2: The railway companies sold land cheaply. Most went to people who wanted to start farms on the Plains. They were called 'homesteaders'. During the 1870s, they flooded into the Plains. They came from as far away as Europe.

Impact 3: The railroads divided the buffalo hunting lands of the Native Americans. So did cattle towns and homesteads. The Native Americans' culture was under threat. The white way of life took over the Plains.

Record

Make your first set of cards. These should remind you:

- when and where railroads spread
- why railroads were built
- how the US government helped railroad companies
- the men who built the railroads
- the impact of railroads on the West:
  - towns
  - land on the Plains
  - Native Americans.

3

▲ A flatcar filled with European immigrants being shown potential farming sites in Kansas

Record

Start your next set of cards. These will be about cattle and ranches. They will need to remind you about:

- the start of cattle ranching in Texas
- the 'cattle trails' to cities
- selling beef to people living on the Plains
- **cow towns** on the Plains
- cowboys and how they lived
- ranches moving into the Plains.

▲ A Texas longhorn

The cattle business

By the 1850s, beef was a popular food in America. Southern Texas became an important centre of cattle ranching. Texas ranchers produced a breed of cattle known as the Texas longhorn. The cattle roamed freely. They grazed on what the cattlemen called 'the open range'. From time to time, cowboys rounded up the cattle into large herds. They drove the herds to markets and cities. By the 1850s, cattlemen had even begun to drive cattle as far as Chicago.

Developing the northern trails

The Civil War stopped the cattle trails for some years. But while cowboys were away fighting, the cattle carried on breeding. By 1865, the herds were huge.

Cattlemen returning from war knew that people in the big cities of the North and East wanted to eat beef. The ranchers hired cowboys and began to organise regular drives to these cities.

Selling beef on the Plains

Cattlemen soon started to use the new railroads which crossed the northern Plains. Now they only had to drive their cattle as far as the towns on the railroads. From there, the cattle could be taken by train to the East.

Fortunes could also be made by selling beef to people on the Plains. It went to:

- Native American **reservations**
- US forts
- railroad builders.

News of the success of Texan ranchers spread rapidly. Soon others were getting in on the action. During the 1870s, the long drives of cattle were a common sight on the Plains.

▲ A map of the main cattle trails and cow towns in the 1870s

Cow towns

In 1867, Joseph McCoy set up the town of Abilene, Kansas. It was right next to the railroad. He told ranchers to bring their cattle to Abilene. From there, the cattle went by rail to the cities of the North and East. Abilene was the first of many cow towns.

Cowboys arrived in the cow towns after weeks on the trail. They might buy a clean set of clothes and head off to a saloon. Many cowboys drank a lot of whisky. They gambled and spent their money on prostitutes. Sometimes there was violence.

In the 1870s, gun laws were introduced. Sheriffs were hired to keep order. The violent cow towns shown in Western films lasted only a few years.

Westerns often fail to show the reality of the cowboy life on the long drive:

- Cowboys worked from dawn until dusk.
- They rode their horses and drove the cattle on the hot, dusty Plains.
- Most were poor young men on low wages.
- Around a third of cowboys were Mexicans, Native Americans or formerly enslaved people.

▼ Dodge City, a cow town, 1878

Reflect
Find the railroad tracks in this photograph of Dodge City.

Cattle ranches move onto the Plains

It was not very efficient to drive cattle from Texas to the cow towns. In 1866, John Iliff, a rancher from Ohio, decided to rear cattle on the Plains instead. This was much closer to the cow towns and the railroad. Other ranchers soon did the same. By the 1870s, cattle ranching had spread across the central Plains.

Ranch owners did not fence the lands they took on the Plains. Cowboys controlled how far the cattle roamed. But cattle on the Plains led to problems such as:

- scarcity of water and grass for buffalo herds
- hunting grounds of Plains Indians were disrupted
- some Native American tribes faced starvation
- violent clashes between ranchers and Native Americans.

By the 1870s, the ranchers were asking the government to send the army to defend their property.

Record
Now use your cards to plan your clear and detailed answer to the question: '**How did the railroads and ranches change the Plains?**'

Make three new 'heading cards'. Use red ink for these. They should say:

- The first towns were built
- New people took the land
- Native Americans suffered

Now choose **only** the cards that help you to explain these three changes. Arrange them beneath the right heading. Keep a photo of your plan.

4.2 How did homesteaders survive and thrive on the Plains?

The cattlemen used the Plains for grazing. They did not grow crops. It was farmers who first turned the Plains into farmland. They were known as 'homesteaders'. In the 1860s and 1870s, hundreds of thousands of homesteaders headed west. They included:

- people who had been freed from slavery in the Southern states
- **immigrants** from Europe
- Americans from the East.

Record

As you read pages 68–71, make a new set of cards. These will be about homesteaders. Pages 69 and 70 give you some hints.

▼ A railroad advertisement for lands in Kansas

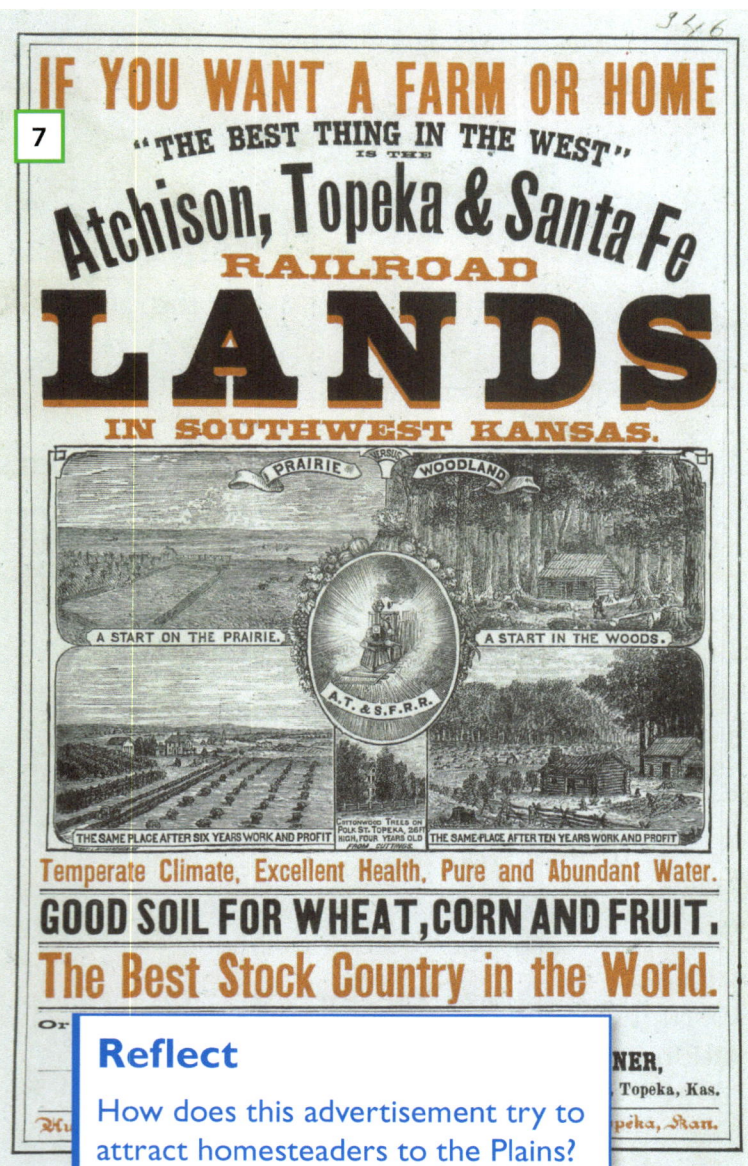

Moving to the Plains

Three factors led to so many people moving onto the Plains after 1861:

Factor 1: Many Americans and European immigrants dreamed of becoming farmers with their own land. Most could only fulfil this dream by buying land on the Plains. It was cheaper there.

Factor 2: In 1862, Lincoln's government introduced the Homestead Act. This Act encouraged people to become land owners. Anyone who paid a small fee would be given 160 acres of Plains land (a homestead). The new owner had to farm it for a full five years. Between 5 and 15 per cent of all these homesteads were owned by women.

Factor 3: Railroad companies wanted people to buy their land. They promoted the West as a land of opportunity. From the 1860s, they began a huge advertising campaign. It ran in Europe as well as in America. You can see an example of a railroad company advertisement on the left.

Reflect

How does this advertisement try to attract homesteaders to the Plains?

Living on the Plains – first steps

Few homesteaders left much evidence of their struggles to survive and thrive on the Plains. One exception is the Oblinger family. Their letters provide a rich record of their lives in the 1870s. It shows their courage and determination. It is worth remembering however that these homesteaders were quite aware that they were settling on lands taken from indigenous peoples. The Oblinger family have left a detailed record of their settlement, but do not mention this issue at all.

The Oblinger family – a case study

Uriah Oblinger set out to Nebraska with his brother in 1872. He left his wife (Mattie) and his young daughter (Ella) back in Indiana. On 6 October 1872, he wrote to them from his new land in Nebraska:

▲ The Oblinger family, c.1870

> Dear Wife & baby
>
> Well, I suppose the first question you would ask me now would be, How do you like Nebraska? Wife … you can see just about as far as you please here. Almost every foot [of land] in sight can be ploughed … The longer I stay, the better I like it.

Over the next year, Uriah built a house. In the spring of 1873, Mattie and Ella came out to join him. They brought all their belongings and a large number of chickens. On 16 June 1873, Mattie wrote to her family back in Indiana:

> Dear Brother & Sister & all of Uncle Wheelers
>
> … we have a good Sunday school in progress now. I suppose there must be about 50 enrolled …
>
> I get milk & butter from Mrs Furgison who lives 1/4 of a mile from us … Most all of the people here live in sod [earth] houses and dug-outs … The one we are in at present is 14 by 16 and a dirt floor …
>
> I wish I had a cow or two to milk, I would feel quite proud …
>
> Uriah has 23 acres of corn. It looks real well. I tell you it is encouraging to have a lot of corn and all your own.

The Oblingers continued to farm their land through the 1870s. Mattie died in childbirth in 1880. Uriah returned to Indiana. A few years later, he remarried and returned to Nebraska. He became a homesteader once again.

Reflect

Compare the Oblinger family's experience with the advertisement on page 68.

Consider, for example:
- land
- house
- health.

Record

Use pages 68–69 to start making your cards about homesteaders. These should remind you:
- what made people want to move West and become homesteaders
- how one family – the Oblingers – coped in their first few years as homesteaders.

Surviving and thriving

In this photograph you can see another homesteader family (the Beckwiths) in front of their Nebraska homestead.

▼ The Beckwith family, Nebraska, 1888

11

> **Reflect**
>
> Find words in the text boxes that match features in this photograph.

> **Record**
>
> Continue making cards about homesteaders. Pages 70–71 are about how homesteaders lived after they had got started.
>
> Make at least one or two cards from each section around the picture.

Keeping healthy

Cleanliness was a major issue for the homesteaders. Most houses had an earth floor and walls, and a grass roof. Mice, fleas and bed bugs were a constant problem.

In the winter, homesteaders could face hardship and hunger. Diseases such as cholera and smallpox were common. The death of a child devastated many families.

Lack of water

Winters on the Plains were freezing. Hot summers often led to droughts. Lack of water was a serious problem for many homesteaders. They needed a regular supply of drinking water. Without water their crops would shrivel and die. Most homesteaders drilled a deep hole into the ground and built a wind pump. This brought water to the surface. You can see the Beckwiths' wind pump in the photograph.

Isolation

Families on the Plains usually lived many miles away from each other. They needed to be tough and independent. As more homesteaders moved onto the Plains, churches and schools were built. Even then, contact with other families was limited.

Ploughing the land

Homesteaders had to plough their land and plant seed. The Plains had never been ploughed before. The grasses which grew there had tough roots. Iron ploughs often broke under the strain. They had to be repaired constantly.

Settlement and conflict on the Plains, 1861–77

Keeping warm
With no wood to burn, it was hard to keep warm in the harsh winters. Their only option was to burn dried buffalo and cow droppings, or 'chips'. They stored these in stacks near the house.

Hazards
In the summer, the grasslands were bone dry. Fire was a real danger. When fire took hold on the Plains, homesteads were destroyed. Families could be forced to give up their holdings. Another hazard was locusts. Between 1874 and 1877, locusts swarmed across parts of the Great Plains. They ate crops and even wooden window frames. A swarm of locust could leave families with no crops to sell.

Fencing the land
Unlike cattlemen, homesteaders needed to fence their property. This showed what land belonged to them. It also stopped cattle from straying into their crops. The lack of timber on the Plains meant that fencing the land was a problem. In 1874, barbed wire was invented. It made fencing cheap and easy.

Building a house
There were very few trees on the prairies. Most homesteaders built sod houses or 'soddies'. These were made from dry blocks of earth (sods). They had grass roofs. In the 1860s and 1870s, most sod houses had holes for windows with simple shutters. They could be cool in summer and warm in winter. However, many leaked or collapsed during storms.

Record
Use your 'homesteaders' cards to plan your answer to the question: '**How did the homesteaders survive and thrive on the Plains?**'

Make these three 'heading cards'. Use red ink for these. They should say:

- Home and family
- Crops and animals
- Overcoming problems

Choose **only** the cards that match these headings. Arrange them beneath the right heading. Explain your choices to a friend. Keep a photo of your plan.

4.3 Why was there so much bloodshed on the Plains, 1861–77?

> **Record**
>
> As you read pages 72–77, make your final set of cards. These are about the US–Lakota Sioux wars that caused so much bloodshed on the Plains, 1861–77.
>
> Page 73 gives you some hints.

Many more ranchers and homesteaders moved into the Plains in the 1860s. Tensions with Native Americans rose. The Native Americans wanted to keep their own way of life on the Plains. In the 1860s and 1870s, they came into bloody conflict with white colonists and the US army. This map shows just some of these clashes.

There were three main factors (reasons) that caused the conflict:

Factor 1: Ecological tensions
The growing number of white colonists created competition for land and water on the Plains. By 1860, this had reached a crisis point.

Factor 2: Hardening attitudes
Many white Americans believed they were better than other races, such as Native Americans. It seemed natural to them that all indigenous peoples should lose their lands. They put pressure on the US government to sign treaties with different tribes. These made Native Americans live on smaller reservations. They had a choice whether to:

- survive on rations supplied by the government, **or**
- take up farming and feed themselves.

Young Native American warriors hated both options. Many formed warrior societies to resist white settlement.

Factor 3: Guns and fear
By the 1850s, it was normal to own handguns. Hunters, farmers and Native Americans all bought Winchester repeating rifles. The Civil War made gun ownership even more common. As fear grew on both sides, guns were used more and more to 'solve' conflicts.

In the period 1861–77, these tensions led to a number of terrible wars on the Plains.

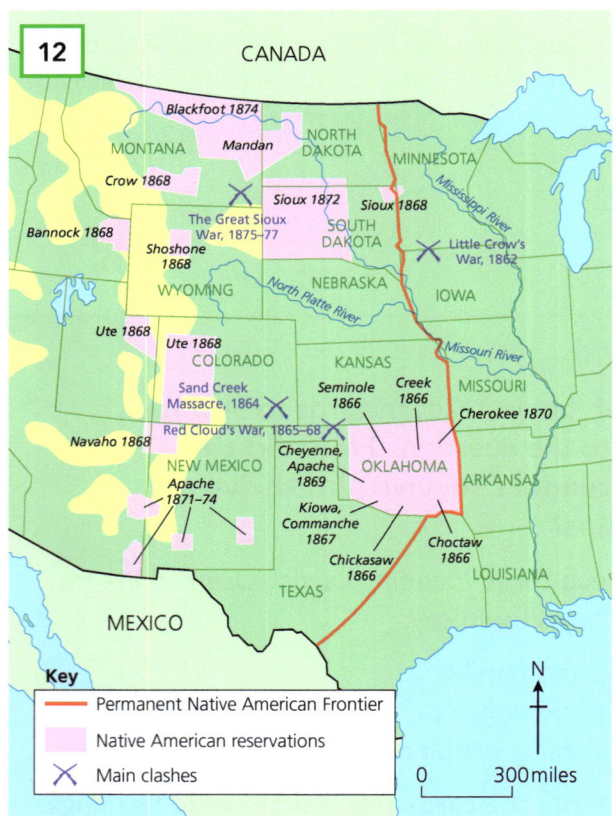

▲ A map showing the main clashes between the Native Americans and the US army, 1861–77

> **Reflect**
>
> 1. Which is the earliest war shown on the map?
> 2. Which is the latest war shown on the map?

Little Crow's War, 1862

By 1861, the Dakota peoples had been forced to give up 28 million acres of land. In exchange they were given a small reservation in southern Minnesota.

Starvation

In the summer of 1862, the Dakota were starving. But the government agent in charge of the reservation refused to open up the emergency stores. Chief Little Crow asked one of the reservation traders to help his people. The trader just said, 'If they are hungry, let them eat grass or their own dung.' The Dakota were furious.

Mass murder

Two days later, Little Crow's followers attacked farms, towns and even army forts. They killed around 500 colonists. The trader whose words had sparked the incident was found dead. His mouth had been stuffed with grass.

The army fought back. On 23 September, the Dakota were defeated. Little Crow escaped but on 3 July 1863, he was shot, beheaded and scalped after a farmer found him picking wild berries.

Revenge

More than 300 Dakota were sentenced to death. Some of their trials lasted only minutes. On Boxing Day 1862, 38 Dakota warriors were hanged in front of a cheering crowd of colonists. Hundreds more were sent to prison. The rest of the tribe was moved to a reservation. But many white colonists were unhappy. They thought that some of the Dakota had got off too lightly.

▲ Little Crow, c.1862

We have continued to use the terms 'Little Crow's War', 'Red Cloud's War' and the 'Great Sioux War' in this section as these are widely used, including in the OCR specification. However, some modern historians suggest that we shouldn't call these 'Indian' wars, because it suggests that Native Americans were to blame for starting them, and as you can see that is not the case. Alternative names for these wars are The US-Dakota War (Little Crow's War), The Powder River War (Red Cloud's War) and The Black Hills War (Great Sioux War).

Record

Use pages 72–73 to start making your cards about the US–Lakota Sioux. These should be about the following:

- Each of the three factors that caused the US–Lakota Sioux wars.
- Little Crow's War, 1862:
  - When it happened
  - Why it happened
  - Main events
  - Results and reactions

▼ The execution of the Dakota warriors in 1862

The Sand Creek Massacre, 1864

> **Record**
> Use pages 74–75 to make more cards. See page 75 for more advice.

After 1858, thousands of miners and colonists moved into Colorado. The US government forced local Cheyenne and Arapaho to leave their lands. They were sent to a very small reservation further east, near Sand Creek.

Hunger at Sand Creek

The reservation's land was poor and they could not grow enough crops. But government agents said they were just lazy. They refused to give them more food.

By 1864, Cheyenne warriors were hunting outside the reservation. They did this to feed their families. Some attacked white settlements. The Governor of Colorado promised to 'kill and destroy' all hostile Native Americans. In September, he set up an army of volunteers to do this. They were called the Third Colorado Volunteers. They could only serve for one hundred days.

The 'Bloodless Third'

Soon after the Volunteers were formed, a Cheyenne chief called Black Kettle said that he wanted to make peace. Native American attacks stopped. But the Governor of Colorado still wanted to kill them. So did the Reverend John Chivington. He was the leader of the Volunteers. People mocked his army for doing no fighting. They called them the 'Bloodless Third'. The chance for blood came when a white colonist was killed by a young Cheyenne warrior. Chivington and 700 Volunteers set out for Sand Creek.

The massacre

At dawn on 29 November, Chivington's troops stormed Black Kettle's camp near Sand Creek.

- Women and children screamed and ran for cover.
- Black Kettle stood in the centre of the camp. He waved an American flag. He believed he had a peace agreement with the white people.
- By mid-morning, 105 Cheyenne women and children and 28 men lay dead.
- Scalps and genitalia were cut from the corpses. Some soldiers kept these as trophies or hat decorations.

Chivington: From hero to villain

At first, Chivington and his men were treated as heroes in Colorado. At a parade in Denver, soldiers marched with Cheyenne people's scalps dangling from their belts. But within a few months the US government launched an investigation. Six of Chivington's men were arrested. Chivington himself was forced to resign from the army.

▲ A Cheyenne fights back at the Sand Creek Massacre. This was painted by Cheyenne warrior-artist, Howling Wolf. He was fifteen years old when he survived the massacre

Red Cloud's War, 1866–68

This is also known as The Powder River War. In 1862, gold was discovered in Montana. The next year, one miner, John Bozeman, set up a new trail into the mining area. This Bozeman Trail ran through the hunting grounds of the Lakota Sioux. This broke the 1851 Fort Laramie Treaty (see page 35). A chain of events followed.

- Red Cloud, Chief of the Lakota Sioux, led attacks on travellers along the Bozeman Trail. These started in 1865.
- The US government sent troops to protect settlers travelling the Bozeman Trail.
- In 1866, the USA called a meeting with Red Cloud at Fort Laramie. The Chief refused to sign a peace treaty.
- The US army set up forts on Lakota Sioux lands without Red Cloud's agreement. The Lakota could not ignore this.

16 ▼ Red Cloud, in a photo from 1880

Victory for the Lakota Sioux

During 1866, Lakota Sioux attacked US army forts. In one attack, they killed an entire troop of 80 US soldiers. They stripped, scalped and cut up the soldiers' bodies.

Red Cloud won many victories in the next two years. In 1868, the US government gave in. At Fort Laramie it agreed a new treaty with the Lakota. This treaty:

- gave the Lakota Sioux a huge area of land, including the Black Hills of Dakota
- promised that US troops and settlers would not enter this land without permission.

Anger in the US army

The 1868 Laramie peace treaty angered politicians and generals. They wanted a tougher policy against the Plains tribes, especially the Lakota Sioux.

In 1868, Generals Sheridan and Sherman were put in charge of the strategy. These were two heroes of the Union army from the Civil War. Sherman wrote to Sheridan in 1868. He made his feelings very clear:

> I ... will use all the powers confided to me to [make sure that] these Indians, the enemies of our race and of our civilisation, shall not again be able to ... carry out their barbarous warfare. 17

Record

Make some cards about the Sand Creek Massacre and Red Cloud's War. For each one, your cards must help you to explain:

- when it happened
- why it happened
- main events
- results and reactions.

18

The Great Sioux War, 1875–77

The most serious of the US–Lakota Sioux was the Great Sioux War (Black Hills War). It was caused by four familiar issues:

> **Record**
> Use pages 76–77 to make cards about the Great Sioux War, 1861–77. As before, these must help you to explain:
> - when it happened
> - why it happened
> - main events
> - results and reactions.

Gold: In 1874, gold was found in the He Sapa (the Black Hills). By 1875, tens of thousands of miners had entered sacred Lakota Sioux lands in Dakota. This broke the 1868 Fort Laramie Treaty.

Treaty: US government officials offered to buy the Black Hills for $6 million. Red Cloud accepted the offer. Another powerful chief, Sitting Bull, did not. He prepared for war.

Vision: In the spring of 1875, Sitting Bull had a vision. As he prayed to the Great Spirit, he saw US troops falling from the sky like dead grasshoppers. He was sure he could win a great victory.

Bloodshed: On 6 June, another Lakota Sioux chief, Crazy Horse, attacked part of the US army. The soldiers were forced to retreat. The victorious Native American warriors joined Sitting Bull.

▲ Sitting Bull, c.1881

The Battle of the Little Bighorn

19

On 21 June 1876, General George Armstrong Custer was ordered to find Sitting Bull's band. He was in charge of the US army's Seventh Cavalry. His orders were to drive Sitting Bull towards the main US army. By this point, there were over 6000 Native Americans at Little Bighorn; 1800 of these were warriors.

On 25 June, Custer surrounded them. He was eager for glory. He charged with 210 cavalrymen into Sitting Bull's camp. The Lakota Sioux were taken by surprise. But within minutes, Crazy Horse was leading a counter-attack. Custer was outnumbered four to one. Many of the white soldiers' weapons overheated or jammed. The frightened cavalry horses bucked and reared, their riders sending shots harmlessly into the air.

▶ General George Armstrong Custer, 1865

Custer finally realised his mistake and ordered a retreat. His men turned their horses and tried to flee back up the slopes. The Lakota Sioux closed in for the kill. One warrior later described his hand-to-hand struggle with one of Custer's men:

> He drew his pistol. I wrenched it out of his hand and struck him with it three or four times on the head ... shot him in the head and fired at his heart ... that was a good fight. **20**

In a matter of hours, it was all over; Custer lay dead along with his entire troop.

Victory and defeat

The Lakota Sioux won a great victory at the Little Bighorn. But they were unable to win the war.

The US army kept them on the run through the winter of 1876. They could not find food or shelter. The government also stopped all rations to the reservations. The Lakota Sioux were forced to sell their land. Crazy Horse was arrested.

He was killed in 1877. A soldier's bayonet was stuck in his back. The army claimed he had tried to escape. Sitting Bull and a small band of followers escaped to Canada. By 1877, all the remaining Lakota Sioux in America had surrendered. The US government illegally took the Black Hills. It had gained a further 40 million acres of Native American land.

▼ Markers of the places where US soldiers were killed at the Little Bighorn National Monument, Montana

21

Record

Use your 'US–Lakota Sioux wars' cards to plan your answer to the question: **'Why was there so much bloodshed on the Plains, 1861–77?'**

Make these four 'heading cards'. Use red ink for these. They should say:

- Land disputes
- Problems on reservations
- Words and actions of individuals
- Violence and revenge

Choose **only** the cards that match these headings. Arrange them beneath the right heading. Explain your choices to a friend. Keep a photo of your plan.

Review

Which of these do you think did most to cause changes that took place on the American Plains between 1861 and 1877:

- The railroads
- The ranchers
- The homesteaders
- The Plains Indians?

CLOSER LOOK 4

Picturing Little Bighorn

The Battle of the Greasy Grass or Little Bighorn was a terrible defeat for the US army, but it was a victory for the Lakota Sioux and the Cheyenne.

The artist Edgar Samuel Paxson spent twenty years researching the battle. He met survivors who gave him eye-witness accounts of what happened. These included US army soldiers and Native American warriors.

In 1895, Paxson started a huge painting of the battle. It took him four years to complete the work. It is six feet by nine feet. He called it 'Custer's Last Stand'.

Paxson and a business partner showed the painting in all the big cities in the east of the USA. They charged people 25 cents each to view it. Paxson boasted that the painting shows:

- exactly the right types of weapons used in the battle
- actual portraits of survivors of the battle.

Reflect

In the painting, find:

- Custer, standing tall in the heart of the battle
- the torn 'Stars and Stripes' flag of the USA
- an army bugler still playing
- Native Americans using guns
- Native Americans using spears or axes.

▼ *Custer's Last Stand*, by Edgar S. Paxson, 1899

22

KEY IDEA 4

Historical significance

Some historical events, people or sources stand out from the rest. We say these have 'historical significance'. There can be different reasons why something is significant (see the panel on the right.)

The table below shows some events from Enquiry 4. We have shown why each one can be called significant.

You could make a table like this for other events in the history of the USA, 1789–1900.

Note that events do not have to match all the four different types of significance.

Events, people or sources may be significant for their:

- **importance** at the time – people remarked on the event as being something special
- **impact** in later years – the consequences of the event shaped later events or our understanding
- **insight** into a situation – such as people's attitudes and values
- **imagery/symbolism** – the way an event or person seems to capture the heart of a situation.

	Historical significance			
Date	Importance at the time	Impact in later years	Insight into attitudes	Imagery: capturing something notable
The Homesteader Act, May 1862	Shows the US government's desire to help farmers settle in the West.	Helped cause mass migration to the West. Speeded up settlement on Native American lands.	Shows the US government's lack of concern for Native American land rights.	
The meeting of the railroads, May 1869	News was sent by telegraph around the world. Seen as a landmark in the growth of the USA. Joined East and West.	Increased trade across USA and into the Pacific.	Shows the confidence of the US government. Shows pride in technology – i.e. steam-powered locomotives.	Captured the imagination of Americans in 1869 just as the moon landing did in 1969.
The Battle of the Little Bighorn, June 1876	Seen as a terrible and shocking defeat.	US army and government showed no mercy after this. Never again did Native Americans defeat the army.	Many white Americans saw Native Americans as savages. Native Americans saw their victory as a sign of hope.	'Custer's Last Stand' has become a symbol of any brave fight against the odds – no matter how foolish.

5 We the people

How did life in the United States change, 1877–1900?

▲ A poster depicting Chicago in the 1890s

> **Reflect**
>
> How does the poster try to show that Chicago was a great and important city?

How did life in the United States change, 1877–1900?

Chicago celebrates America's achievements

In 1892, the city of Chicago started to create a huge exhibition. Its site covered 600 acres. Over 27 million people visited this 'World's Fair' after it opened in 1893.

The fair aimed to promote American technology and culture. Visitors could admire America's latest steam-powered machines and electrical goods.

They could also marvel at Chicago's wide streets and towering buildings. The city claimed to be just as 'civilised' as Paris, London or Berlin.

Whose America?

Some Americans were not really on show at the World's Fair.

- Black Americans were not even allowed to help build the fair. None were shown on any of the American stands. Black leaders said the fair ignored black contributions to the USA.
- Native Americans hardly appeared in the exhibition. The few who did appear were shown as an interesting sideshow.

The opening words of the US Constitution are 'We the people'. At Chicago's World Fair of 1893, the only Americans who seemed to matter were white.

▼ A photograph of Chicago's Home Insurance Building shortly after it opened in 1884. This was the world's first skyscraper

The Enquiry

Between 1877 and 1900 the United States became one of the world's leading industrial nations. For many Americans it was a period of advancement and prosperity, but others were left behind as America surged forward.

In this Enquiry you will examine exactly how the United States changed between 1877 and 1900 and the impact this had on different groups of Americans. Your challenge is to plan a new exhibition called 'How life in the United States changed, 1877–1900'.

The exhibition will be in three parts:

1. The changing lives of indigenous peoples
2. The changing lives of black Americans
3. The growth of big business, cities and mass migration.

For each part of the exhibition, you will:

- gather notes about the changes
- write a short introduction or conclusion panel for visitors to the exhibition
- select a picture to be the 'lead image' and provide visitors with the context for this.

5.1 The lives of the indigenous peoples, 1877–1900

By 1877, almost all indigenous peoples lived on reservations. There were four main reasons for this.

Record

See the advice on page 83. It will help you as you prepare to make your first exhibition panel.

Reason 1: Military defeat

The Battle of Greasy Grass in 1876 was only a short-term success for the Lakota Sioux. By 1881, Sitting Bull had surrendered. He and his people were forced to live on the Standing Rock Reservation in South Dakota. Like other defeated tribes, their hope of a victory over the US army had gone. They could not go back to their old way of life.

Reason 2: The destruction of the buffalo

As the railroads spread west, they opened up the Plains. Hunters used the railroad to reach the millions of buffalo who lived there. They made money by selling buffalo hides, meat and bones. The skulls and bones were ground up and used as a fertiliser. Buffalo were slaughtered in their thousands. A single hunter could kill over a hundred buffalo a day.

The US army encouraged buffalo hunting. It would take away the food supplies of Plains tribes. They hoped this would force them onto reservations. It did.

By 1883, the vast herds of the 1840s were all but gone.

3

Reflect

Why was this great pile of buffalo skulls of any value to hunters?

Reservations and the attempted destruction of indigenous cultures and peoples

Military defeat and the loss of the buffalo are not the only reasons why Native Americans moved onto reservations. Here are two more:

Reason 3: Fences and factories
- White cattle ranchers fenced off large areas in the south-west. Pueblo people used to keep sheep on that land. Without grass, the Pueblo herds soon died out.
- Homesteaders fenced off their water supplies. This meant indigenous peoples could no longer roam freely on the Plains as their horses had no water.
- Canning factories grew up in western cities. These paid people to go to the Plains and pick berries and other wild foods. Soon the nomadic indigenous tribes could not find the food they needed on the Plains.

Reason 4: US policies divide the tribes
In the late 1870s, the US government deliberately split up the tribes. They did this to weaken them.
- The Lakota Sioux and Dakota people were divided over at least five major reservations.
- The Nez Perce tribe of Oregon were moved over 2000 miles to a reservation in Oklahoma.
- Other tribes were made to share reservations. Over time, each tribe lost its ancient identity.

Finding food on the reservations

Once the indgenous peoples were living on reservations, life changed. From the late 1870s, the government banned them from hunting outside reservations. They were encouraged to grow corn and squash on reservation land. These crops struggled to grow in the harsh Plains conditions. Many indigenous peoples living on reservations had to depend on government beef rations to survive. They were no longer independent. Poverty, hunger and disease haunted the lives of many Native Americans.

▼ Lakota Sioux line up in front of a barn on a reservation to receive their beef rations, c.1893

Record

Part of this exhibition display will be a large diagram. It will look like this:

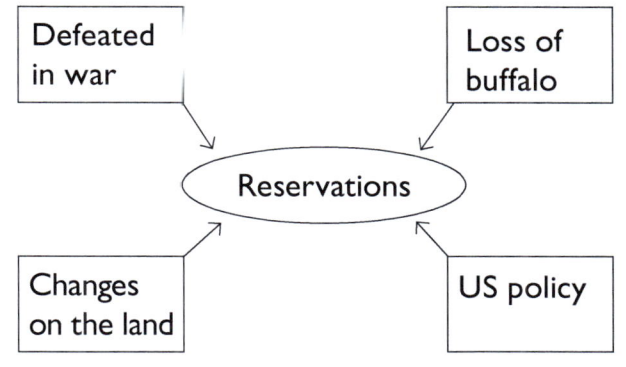

Why so many Native Americans lived on reservations 1877–1900

Write the text for each of the 'Reasons' boxes. Explain clearly why that reason caused Native Americans to move to reservations. Use the green panels on pages 82–83 to help you.

Deliberate attempted destruction of indigenous cultures

Between 1877 and 1900, the US government deliberately tried to destroy Native American culture. This box shows some of the ways it did this.

1. Indigenous peoples were made to give up their old ways of ruling themselves. The new ways were similar to those used by the US government.
2. Nomadic peoples like the Lakota Sioux or Apache were encouraged to live in houses and lodges instead of tipis.
3. Most indigenous peoples were made to become Christians. They could be arrested and imprisoned if they kept up their religious beliefs and customs.
4. Some children were sent away to residential schools. These were run by white Americans. The children could be beaten if they spoke their own languages at school. Girls were taught to sew and play the piano. Boys were taught to read and write.
5. Children who went to school had to change their names. They sometimes chose their new name from a list written on a blackboard.

▼ (Left) A group of Apache arriving at the Carlisle Indian Industrial School in 1890. (Right) The same group four months later

Record

The next exhibition panel will be called '**The attempted destruction of indigenous cultures**'.

From pages 83 and 84 make brief notes under the following headings:

- Problems finding food
- Deliberate destruction by the US government
- The work of the 'Friends'

Under your notes, explain which of these three did most harm to Native American culture. Use details to support your answer.

The 'Friends of the Indian'

In 1883, a group of white Americans formed a group called 'Friends of the Indian'. It aimed to help Native Americans.

- It rooted out corrupt agents. These men took government money – but did not use it to help reservation Indians.
- It set up 'better' residential schools. In 1889, one former student became the first female Native American doctor in the USA.
- It persuaded the government to pass the Dawes Act in 1887. This offered individual Native Americans 160 acres of land and full US citizenship. In return, they gave up their right to hold tribal land. By 1900, nearly two-thirds of the land that Native American tribes had held in 1877 was owned by white Americans. They could never regain their old lands.

A final vision for freedom – the Ghost Dance

Some Native Americans refused to accept the changes being demanded by white Americans. In the 1890s, a new religion, the Ghost Dance, was sweeping the reservations of the American West. These Ghost Dancers believed that if they danced and prayed for long enough, a saviour would come to them. He would return the buffalo and sweep white people from the land like a great flood.

White Americans living near reservations were really worried. A rumour began that Sitting Bull was planning to join the Ghost Dancers.

The US army was sent in to arrest the Ghost Dancers. During the process, Lakota Sioux police were told to go and arrest Sitting Bull. Forty policemen burst into the chief's cabin. They dragged him out into the snow and shot him through the skull.

A final disaster – Wounded Knee

The remaining Ghost Dancers tried to escape. General Miles and the Seventh Cavalry set out to find them.

On 29 December 1890, Miles found the Ghost Dancers at a place called Wounded Knee. They were largely defenceless. Children played as the cavalry moved in to disarm the Native Americans. A shot was fired. In response, Miles ordered his troops to open fire. Cannon were rolled out. They bombarded the Ghost Dancers.

The smoke cleared. The children who had been playing just minutes before now lay dead. Their bodies were loaded into a mass grave along with over 250 other men, women and children who had been cut down in the massacre. On 15 January 1891, the remaining 4000 Ghost Dancers surrendered.

> **Record**
>
> The next exhibition panel will be called **'Six things you should know about the Ghost Dance and Wounded Knee, 1890–91'**.
>
> Use this page to write down what you think those six statements should say.

> **Reflect**
>
> Look back at all the pictures on pages 82–85. Decide which you will use as the 'lead image' for your exhibition. For each one, consider the advantages and disadvantages.

> **Record**
>
> 1 Write your short introduction to the exhibition's section on **'How the lives of Native Americans changed, 1877–1900'**.
> 2 Say which picture you have chosen as your 'lead image'. Write a short piece of text to tell visitors what they need to know to understand the image.

5.2 The changing lives of black Americans, 1877–1900

The next four pages tell you about:

- economic changes – these are to do with money
- social changes – these are to do with how people live
- political changes – these are to do with people's rights and power.

In the 1890s, civil rights campaigners like Ida Wells and Frederick Douglass tried hard to improve all these aspects of life for black Americans. Douglass died in 1895, but Ida Wells continued her remarkable campaign for civil rights.

Ida Wells

▲ Civil rights and anti-lynching campaigner, Ida Wells

Ida Wells had been born into slavery in 1862. From 1865 she was free and she did well at school. She became a teacher.

In 1884, her life changed. She was travelling first class on a train. The train staff ordered her to move to a carriage for black Americans. She protested. When one of the train crew tried to move her she bit him on the hand. She sued the train company but lost the case. Ida was furious.

From that day on, Ida spent the rest of her life telling the wider public about the unfairness of life for black Americans.

Ida became a journalist. She travelled all over the USA. The three main subjects she wrote about were:

- the poor quality of education received by black children
- the growing problem of lynching (this means the murder of black Americans by white racists)
- the great contributions black Americans were making to the USA.

Record

For this part of the Enquiry, you must sort your notes into two columns as shown in the table below. You will need to find examples from pages 86–89 to write in the two columns. We have started your table for you.

The changing lives of black Americans, 1877–1900	
Improvements	Challenges
Campaigners like Ida Wells stood up for black American rights by … [add extra details]	Racist laws continued, e.g. 1884, Ida Wells had to travel in a 'blacks only' carriage.

How did life in the United States change, 1877–1900?

Economic changes, 1877–1900

America's economy generally improved in this period. This helped some black Americans. But most still lived in poverty.

> **Reflect**
> Where in the USA do you think an black American might find good work:
> - the South
> - the West
> - the North?

Life in the South

After the Civil War, the cotton trade was very slow to recover. The wages paid to cotton workers stayed very low. By 1900, Southern income was half that of the North. Black Americans were free, but they were often trapped in low-paid work. Most were still poor sharecroppers. They worked on plantations owned by former slave holders.

Opportunities in the West

In 1877, an ex-slave called Benjamin Singleton started an 'exodus' (great departure) of black people from the South. He wanted them to move west, away from white violence. He urged people who had been enslaved to claim government land promised in the Homestead Act (see page 68). Thousands followed him to Kansas. They became known as the 'Exodusters'.

▼ An Exoduster family on their Kansas homestead, 1887

Challenges in the North

Between 1877 and 1900, many black Americans left the Southern states. They went to find work in the growing industrial cities of the North. This was not always easy.

- Black workers often saw jobs go to less skilled white labourers.
- In the North, white people were upset when black people took jobs or houses that they wanted.
- Business owners sometimes used black workers when white people went on strike.

This all added to the bad feeling between black and white people.

Education and training

Booker T. Washington was another leader of black Americans. In 1882, he set up a school for black students. Boys learned practical skills such as farming. Girls learned how to be good housekeepers or servants. Washington set up many more schools. They helped to lift some black Southerners out of poverty. Some went on to do very well: by 1900, America had 23,866 black teachers, 417 black doctors and 300 black lawyers.

▼ Booker T. Washington, c.1910

87

> **Record**
>
> Use pages 88–89 to add more notes to your 'Improvements and Challenges' table.

Social changes, 1877–1900

Daily life for most black Americans was harsh. Somehow they had to try to cope with these social problems.

The Jim Crow laws

In the 1890s, many Southern states passed laws to keep black and white people apart. They became known as the Jim Crow laws.

The laws segregated (kept apart) black and white people in places like trains, shops, churches, parks and even schools. White schools received ten times as much funding as black ones. In 1896, the Supreme Court agreed that it was legal to segregate the races like this.

Black churches

After the Civil War, black Americans were allowed to start their own churches in the South. By 1900, there were 26 black bishops. Black churches became very popular. Their members built up a strong sense of community. However, many preachers did little to challenge the Jim Crow laws.

Living conditions

In the South the amount of land owned by black Americans tripled between 1877 and 1900. However, the houses on this land were usually very poor. In the North, many black migrants also grouped together in poor districts. The quality of housing in these areas was often terrible. Racist landlords would not let black people move into better homes.

▼ Poor-quality housing on the edge of New York, 1890s

Black academics and artists

Academics are highly qualified university teachers. By 1900, a group of black academics emerged in the North. William DuBois was one of these. He became a history professor at Atlanta University. Black-American musicians, writers and artists also began to do well.

> **Reflect**
>
> Which do you think did more to help African Americans?
> - Church and religion
> - Owning a house and some land
> - Art and music

How did life in the United States change, 1877–1900?

Political changes, 1877–1900

Black Americans had very little power in these years.

The Redeemers

Most governments in the South at this time were run by ex-slave holders. They called themselves 'Redeemers' (saviours). They tried to 'save' the South by limiting the rights of black Americans. In the 1890s, new state laws said people in the South could only vote if they first passed a literacy test. Many thousands of black people could not read or write well. They were banned from voting.

The Ku Klux Klan

The Ku Klux Klan (KKK) was a violent, white group. It used terror to oppress black people in the South. By the early 1870s, the US government had stopped most KKK activity. In the 1890s, the KKK secretly re-formed. Black Americans in the South lived in fear of its terrifying threats and brutal violence. They had no power to stop it.

Constitutional changes

The South continued to ignore the rights of black Americans. Campaigners like Ida Wells did not give up. They used Amendments that had been made to the Constitution to demand equality. They showed that black Americans could never again be held as enslaved people. They managed to make Southern states agree to provide a basic education and other support (e.g. transport) for black Americans.

Lynching

After 1870, groups of white people carried out their own mob 'justice'. They lynched (murdered) black people. They might think their black victim had been insulting or simply was too wealthy. In 1892 alone, 161 black citizens were lynched. They were often tortured first. Their bones were broken, flesh cut and their skin burned. Hardly any of the white mobs were arrested.

Record

This time you must prepare a conclusion panel for this part of the exhibition. It should look like this. It shows a set of scales. Above the scales are two lists.

- One shows five significant improvements for black Americans, 1877–1900.
- The other shows five significant challenges.

The visitors will be challenged to 'weigh up' the evidence in the two lists. They then decide which list outweighs the other: improvements or challenges?

1 From your own lists, choose the **five most important improvements** and **five most important challenges**. Write them onto a simple copy of this diagram.
2 Choose a picture from pages 86–89 to display next to the diagram. Write a short piece of text to tell visitors what they need to know to understand the image.

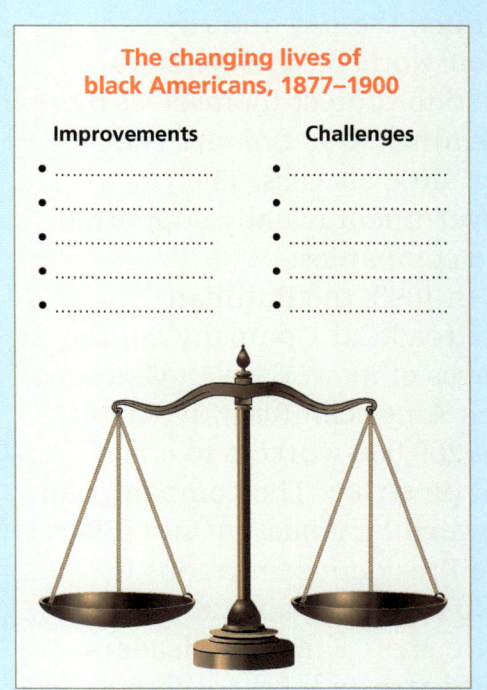

The changing lives of black Americans, 1877–1900

5.3 The impact of big business, cities and mass migration on America

Record

See the advice at the end of page 91.

Big business

This is Andrew Carnegie. As a poor Scottish boy he moved to America in 1848. He started work as a telegraph operator. By 1901, he was the billionaire head of a steel-making corporation. He had worked hard and invested well. In his last years he gave more than 90 per cent of his wealth to charities. Carnegie's story is just one example of American big business success.

The growth of big corporations

Traditional American businesses were owned by a single person or family. Between 1877 and 1900 this changed. Mighty corporations, like the one run by Carnegie, were created. These were run by a president and a board of shareholders.

Around 1850, there were 5300 manufacturing firms in the USA. By the end of the century they had been absorbed by just 334 corporations.

▲ Andrew Carnegie, 1905

The workers

These huge corporations limited the pay and rights of their workers. The workers tried to protect themselves by forming **trade unions**. They had little success. The US government usually supported the companies.

In 1893, the Pullman Railroad Car Company cut the wages of its workers in Chicago. The American Railway Union got 260,000 workers to come out on strike. The company had powerful friends. In July 1894, the President sent troops to stop the strike and 26 workers were shot. The strike leaders were arrested. Few of them were able to find work again.

Reflect

How is this cartoon useful for a historian studying American big business in 1883?

▲ A cartoon commenting on how American industrialists treated their workers, 1883

How did life in the United States change, 1877–1900?

Three important branches of America's big business

Business type	Nature of the business	Impact of the business
Cotton and tobacco factories	Before 1880 the South never made cotton cloth. It just sent raw cotton to the North or Europe. By 1900, it produced more cloth than the North. Tobacco production increased dramatically. By 1904, the American Tobacco Company controlled 90 per cent of cigarette production.	The rise of cotton factories did not help poor cotton pickers. Their wages were so low that they could barely survive. For white Southerners, new jobs were created in the cotton and tobacco factories. Most of these were low-skilled and poorly paid.
Fossil fuels and mineral extraction (mining)	As factories and railroads grew, they needed vast amounts of coal and iron. Small mining could not cope so huge mining operations stepped in. In the South, coal production increased ten times between 1875 and 1890. Companies also ran copper, tin, lead and silver mines.	Mining damaged the environment. Huge areas of forest were cut down to create supports for mine shafts. Chemicals polluted the water supply. The impact on indigenous populations in mining areas was severe. Mining was dangerous. Mine shafts sometimes collapsed. Many miners died of lung diseases.
Bonanza farms and cattle ranches	In the 1880s, huge 'bonanza' farms appeared on the Plains. Their average size was 10,000 acres. Most were owned by rich groups in eastern cities. They paid their farm workers very low wages. Bonanza cattle ranches also developed. Bigger ranches bought up smaller ones. By 1900, most ranches in the West were owned by just a handful of people.	Bonanza farms often had the best land, water supplies and railroad links. It became nearly impossible for small-scale farms to survive. Many farmers moved to the cities or became wage workers on a bonanza farm. Farming and ranching had a terrible impact on the environment. They used up the limited supplies of water. This forced even more Native Americans off the land and onto reservations.

Record

Make a large copy of this 'Big Changes' table (right). Leave enough room in each row to add your own notes. Use pages 90–91 to complete the column about big business.

- In the 'Developments' box, describe how business was changing.
- In the 'Impact' box, explain how those changes affected the USA.

	Big business	Big cities	Big migration
	Developments:	Developments:	Developments:
	Impact:	Impact:	Impact:

The growth of cities

> **Record**
>
> As you read page 92, complete the middle column of your 'Big Changes' table (see page 91).

In 1870, the USA had just fourteen cities with populations over 100,000. By 1900, there were 38. These great cities became home to new immigrants, failed homesteaders and black Americans fleeing the South. Chicago is a fine example of how and why cities grew.

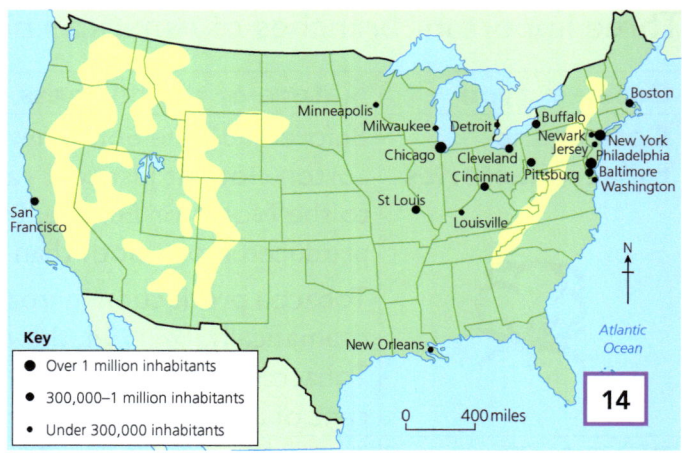

▲ A map showing the main American cities in 1900

Chicago is situated on Lake Michigan. It is also close to the Mississippi River. This made it a great transport hub. It became America's railroad centre. People found jobs in transport, factories, shops or banks. Chicago's population went from 200 in 1833, to 300,000 in 1870. By 1900, it was over 1.5 million.

After a huge fire in 1871, much of Chicago was rebuilt in steel and stone. In 1884, the city put up the world's first steel-frame skyscraper.

> **Reflect**
>
> Why did American cities keep growing between 1877 and 1900?

The impact of cities on jobs and lives

During the 1880s, the elevator (lift) was invented. This allowed cities to build ever-taller skyscrapers. This created more demand for iron, steel, coal. That created even more new jobs. Migrants moved in with great hopes. They had mixed experiences:

Difficulties in cities
- Most lived in poorly designed, overcrowded apartments.
- There was little privacy.
- Sanitation was often poor.
- Death rates of children in cities were very high.

Delights in cities
- Citizens enjoyed theatres, parks and saloons.
- They could attend political meetings and choose between dozens of newspapers.
- By 1900, 70 per cent of children went to school.
- Women, too, had greater freedom in the city. In the West, they began to demand the right to vote.

▲ A panoramic view of Chicago, c.1900

How did life in the United States change, 1877–1900?

Mass migration to America

By 1880, America's economy was recovering from the Civil War. This led to a surge in migration. New steam-powered ships had low fares. It became easier to move from Europe.

Migrants poured into the USA at the end of the nineteenth century. Most came from central, eastern or southern Europe. In the 1890s, 600,000 came from Italy alone.

At first, the US government allowed individual states to decide how many migrants to take. By 1890, so many were arriving that the federal government took control. Two years later it opened America's main immigration station on Ellis Island, New York.

> **Record**
>
> As you read page 93, complete the final column of your 'Big Changes' table (see page 91).

The migrant experience – arrival

As migrants sailed into New York harbour, they would see the Statue of Liberty. It was as if she was offering new lives of freedom and prosperity. That was the 'American Dream'.

At the Ellis Island Immigration Centre migrants were given a medical test. Around 10 per cent of people were too unwell to enter the USA straight away. They were taken to a hospital on the island.

Healthy migrants went by ferry to New York. Some settled in the city, but most headed west where they hoped to build their new lives.

16

▲ Immigrants arriving in America

The migrant impact on America

Over 7 million migrants reached America in these years. Most did well in the end. Some owned farms or shops. Far more worked in factories. They helped to build America's great wealth. But their arrival also added to America's social problems.

- In some cities there was anti-immigrant violence. Desperate migrants would work for lower wages. White workers were pushed out of jobs in favour of migrants.
- Migrants sometimes faced prejudice, particularly Catholics and Jewish people.
- In the West there were anti-Chinese riots and murders in the 1870s. Chinese people made up 10 per cent of the population of San Francisco. In 1882, the US government passed an Act that limited the number of Chinese people that could enter America.

> **Record**
>
> 1. Write your short introduction to the exhibition's section on '**The growth of big business, cities and mass migration, 1877–1900**'.
> 2. Choose a picture to be the 'lead image' for this part of the exhibition. It can be from pages 90–93 or from an image search. Write a short piece of text to tell visitors what they need to know to understand the image.

CLOSER LOOK 5

Quanah Parker: One man, many visions

This is Quanah Parker of the Comanche. His remarkable and unusual life went through these five stages.

The white woman's son

Quanah's mother was a white American. She was kidnapped as a child by some Comanche people. She grew up among them and married a Comanche chief. She gave birth to her son, Quanah, around 1850.

The leader of the Comanche

Quanah became a Comanche chief. In 1867, he refused to accept a treaty that would have confined his people to a reservation. Instead he led his people in a brutal war against the Texans. This lasted until 1874 when Quanah and his Comanche were forced to surrender. They were moved onto a reservation.

The 'tamed' Comanche

Quanah became the leader of all Comanche on the reservation. He built himself a house and began using his white surname, Parker. He also learned to speak English. He was taking on the white vision of the West. However, he still wore his hair in braids and never accepted Christianity.

The modern American

By the 1880s, Parker invested $40,000 in a new railway. This made him one of the wealthiest Native Americans of all time. His reputation and wealth helped him become a friend of President Theodore Roosevelt. He used this friendship to lobby the government on behalf of the Comanche.

The traitor to his people?

In 1892, Parker signed an agreement which broke up the Comanche reservation and gave each Comanche their own small parcel of land. He believed that the Comanche needed to adapt to survive. Other Comanche believed that he was a traitor who was selling his people out to a white enemy.

17

Reflect

Which part of Quanah Parker's life do you find most remarkable?

KEY IDEA 5

Diversity between and within groups

Quanah Parker was a most unusual man. Most people would find it hard to imagine that a Comanche warrior could become the wealthy friend of a US president. History is very rarely neat and tidy. It is full of diversity (differences).

In this book you have learned that it is too simple to talk about 'Americans' as if they were all the same. You have studied three main groups. These are:

- white Americans
- black Americans
- Native Americans.

It is good to remember this diversity in American society. But we have to go further. We need to remember that there is diversity *within* each group. The diagram below summarises some aspects of this diversity in the period 1877–1900.

Within each circle you can see examples of people from each of the three main groups. Next to each is a page reference. If you look back at those pages you will see just how diverse their lives were.

You could create similar review diagrams for the other periods covered in the book.

Diversity within American society, 1877–1900

Native Americans
- Quanah Parker, a wealthy Commanche businessman – **p94**
- A 'Ghost Dancer' shot down at Wounded Knee – **p85**
- A Lakota Sioux woman queuing for food rations – **p83**, photograph
- The first Native American woman to qualify as a doctor – **p84**

Black Americans
- An 'Exoduster' family farming their own land – **p87**
- Black city workers, living in slum areas – **p88**
- A victim of a Ku Klux Klan lynching in the Deep South – **p89**
- Educated black leaders like Ida Wells and Booker T. Washington – **pp86–7**

White Americans
- Members of the KKK – **p89**
- Members of the 'Friends of the Indian' – **p84**
- Billionaire and corporation boss, Andrew Carnegie – **p90**
- A striker demanding better pay in Carnegie's steel mills – **p90**
- Migrants from Europe and Asia with different languages, religions and skills – **p93**

Preparing for the examination

The following show five methods for making summary notes. We have provided a different model for each enquiry. Some are more detailed than others. Choose the method you prefer and make your own summaries of all five sections of the course.

Method 1: Mind map – America's expansion, 1789–1838

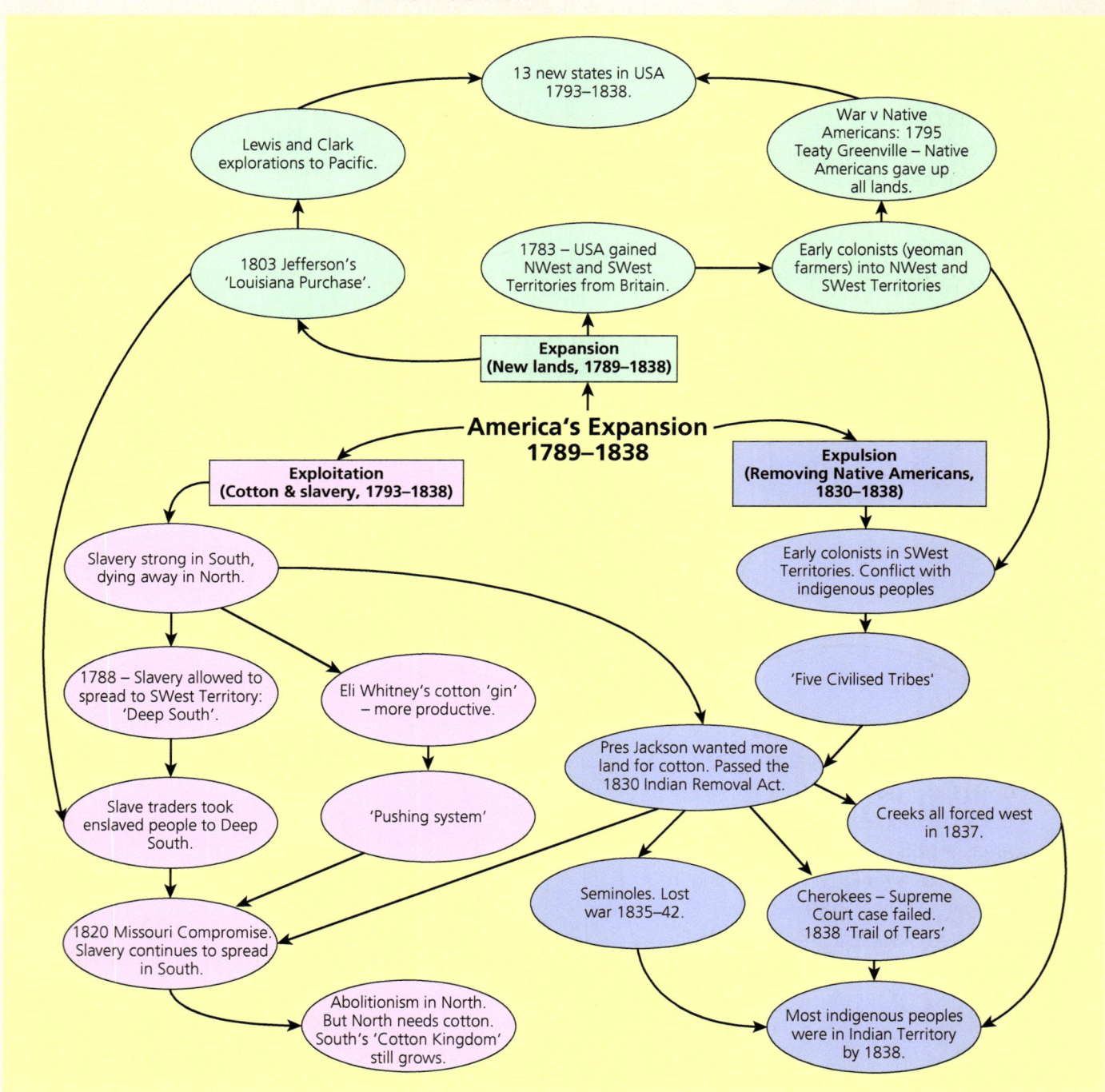

Method 2: Small cards – the West, 1839–60

Cards can be re-arranged by themes, for example the causes of migration west or the impact of migration on Native Americans.

Native Americans (Mainly Lakota Sioux)

Overview
- Many tribes
- Nomads
- Hunted buffalo
- 'Great Spirit'

Buffalo provided
- Meat for food
- Skins/fur for clothes, tipis
- Bone for tools

Tipis
- Easy to move
- Practical
- Strong in winds

Roles
- Men: hunt, fight
- Women: cook, make clothes, move tipis
- Children: valued, learned skills
- Aged: respected but allowed to die when struggling

Beliefs
- Great Spirit
- Rocks, streams all have spirit
- Circles, e.g. sun valued
- Land not owned
- He Sapa (the Black Hills) sacred

Leaders/war
- No single chief
- Bands have chiefs
- Fought other tribes for hunting land
- 'Warrior bands' like teams – very proud

Colonists

Reasons to move west
- Trade slump 1837–46
- Advertisements
- Oregon land law
- 'Manifest Destiny'
- Routes opened

Journey west – basics
- c.2400 miles max.
- c.8 months
- Included Europeans, black Americans

Journey – evidence from
- Diaries, e.g. Abigail Scott, Catherine Sager

Journey – main challenges
- Heat and cold
- Empty Plains, high mountains
- Some hostile Native Americans
- Accidents, e.g. wagons
- Disease, e.g. cholera and measles

Journey – helped by
- Army forts and treaties with indigenous peoples
- Native American guides, supplies
- Careful planning
- Faith in God
- Luck

Impact on Native Americans
- Guided/traded
- Hunting grounds disturbed by routes
- Wars with other tribes over hunting lands
- Lost land in Oregon/California

Mormons

Mormon origins
- Founded 1830 by Joseph Smith
- 'Book of Mormon'
- Wanted to start perfect new church in USA

Mormons unpopular for
- Sharing land/property
- Very powerful leaders
- Too keen to convert
- Allowed polygamy

Mormons went west as
- Wanted own 'Holy City'
- Nauvoo failed, 1846

Brigham Young
- Mormon leader after Smith murdered, 1844
- Very strong leader
- 55 wives
- Knew of no other settlers at Salt Lake, Utah

Salt Lake City
- Founded in 1847
- c.10,000 Mormons there by 1852
- All land shared out
- Grew by hard work
- Water channelled from mountains

Mormon problems in Utah
- Marriage and land rules broke US law
- Gov't feared spread of Mormon faith
- 1857 – B. Young no longer governor when settlers killed

Miners

Origins in California
- Gold found in Sierra Nevada, Jan 1848
- Rumours spread
- Gold diggers rush in
- Official by Dec 1848

1849 Gold Rush
- c.50,000 people
- By land and sea
- From East, Europe, China, Mexico

Non-mining profits
- Traders sell tools, etc.
- Cooks, washerwomen
- Clothes, e.g. Levi jeans

California after 1849
- Mining companies – miners on low wages
- Machinery/chemicals cut and clean rock
- Population grew so became state in 1850
- Wanted rail link east
- Polluted rivers/land
- Some Native Americans were enslaved

Pike's Peak
- Gold found in 1858 in Rocky Mts, Colorado
- c.100,000 people moved in by 1859
- Rail links from East helped access
- 'Town boosters'

Pike's Peak impact
- Farms/towns grew on Plains to supply mines
- Native American hunting lands being taken by white colonists
- Tension between Native Americans and colonists

Method 3: Charts – Civil War and Reconstruction, 1861–77

Divisions over slavery/causes of the Civil War	Black American Experience of war	Reconstruction

• Pre-war South:
  – Little industry, many plantations, relied on c.3.2 million unpaid enslaved people
• Pre-war North:
  – Mainly industry and trade. Relied on low-paid free labourers
  – Still needed raw cotton from South
• Abolitionist views spread by:
  – W.L. Garrison's *Liberator* newspaper
  – ex-slaves speakers, for example Frederick Douglass, Harriet Tubman
  – anti-slavery novel 'Uncle Tom's cabin' 1851
• 1850: 'Clay Compromise' allowed slavery in California if people voted for it
• 1854, Kansas–Nebraska Act: slavery to be allowed in these states if people voted for it. Violence as people moved in to sway the vote
• November 1860: Abraham Lincoln (Republican) won election to be president: promised to stop slavery spreading
• November 1860: S Carolina voted to leave USA (the Union)
• By early 1861, six more Southern States left Union
• February 1861: Confederate states (the South) elected own president, Jefferson Davis
• April 1861: Confederate troops attacked Union troops at Fort Sumter (Charleston). Civil War started
	Phase 1: 'Limited war':
	• In South, much as before:
	  – Enslaved people work on plantations
	  – Not allowed to read/write
	  – Cannot share public spaces with white people
	  – A few worked for army but not as soldiers
	• In North, much as before:
	  – Black Americans mainly in poor jobs, low-paid, bad housing in cities
	  – A few were well-educated
	  – All segregated (separate) from white people in public
	  – Could not serve in army
	  – Enslaved people freed in early part of war were 'contrabands': not freed but could, for example, work for Union army, not as soldiers
	  – 1862: New law said all enslaved people on plantations captured by Union were to be freed.
	Phase 2: 'Total War':
	• 1 Jan 1863: Lincoln said all enslaved people would be set free if Union won war
	• Autumn 1862: Black Americans allowed to fight in Union army
	• Some racism in Union army, for example pay and work duties
	• North supported ex-slaves in South, for example education, land grants
	• 1863: New York riots/lynchings by angry white men
		• 13th Amendment – Jan 1865: no slavery in USA
		• 9 April 1865, South beaten
		• Lincoln killed, April 1865
		• Andrew Johnson – new president. Soft on South
		• Old leaders back in power in South. Pass 'Black Codes' to take away black American rights
		• 1866 Republican Congress helped ex-slaves: led by 'Radicals'
		• Set up Freedman's Bureau to give land to ex-slaves
		• June 1866: 14th Amendment: all people born in USA – full citizens
		• 1867: US army put in charge of South
		• 1868: New President Grant. Helped ex-slaves at first. Stopped later
		• 1868: many black men in state governments in South
		• 1869: 15th Amendment: all races have right to vote
		• 1870: Republicans lost control of Congress
		• Ku Klux Klan and White League violence stopped ex-slaves voting
		• 1873: Supreme Court allowed segregation of races
		• 1875: Supreme Court said federal government has no power to protect black American voters in South

Method 4: Parallel timelines – settlement and conflict on the Plains, 1861–77

Year	Railroads and Ranches	Homesteaders	Bloodshed US–Lakota Sioux wars
Before 1861	Cattle ranching in Texas. Open range. Cattle trails, e.g. Chicago	Cheap land available in West	Competition for land/water Attitudes: white people felt 'superior' Guns – available, e.g. Winchester
1861			
1862	Lincoln: Pacific Railroad Act – Money and land to railroad companies. Ended treaties on Native Americans' land rights	Pres Lincoln passed Homestead Act: encouraged new farms on Plains	**Little Crow's War 1862** Dakota people on Minnesota reservation. Dakota starving: attacked forts/farms 23 Sep: Dakota defeated. Little Crow fled 38 Dakota hanged. Rest to Dakota
1863			3 July – Little Crow shot, beheaded
1864	$50m Gov't funds to go to companies that would build railroad across USA		**Sand Creek Massacre – 1864** Cheyenne hungry. Raids killed white people Third Cavalry Volunteers –'Bloodless Third' 29 Nov – Chivington attack at Sand Creek. Killed 105 women/children and 28 men
1865	Railroad under way – 12,000 Chinese tunnel mountains Others on Plains – harsh Huge cattle herds after Civil War Northern trails now to railroads		Chivington tried. Resigned
1866	John Iliff – first ranch on Plains. Ranches spread: clashed with Native American buffalo hunting lands		US army forts on Lakota Sioux lands broke treaty **Red Cloud's War 1866–68** Miners – Bozeman Trail to gold fields. Broke Laramie Treaty Red Cloud (Lakota Sioux) attacked miners Red Cloud attacks kill 80 soldiers
1867	Abilene first cow town: Joseph McCoy		More Red Cloud successful attacks
1868	Early, violent days of cow towns Cowboys – young, worked hard 30% Mexican, Native American, ex-slaves		New Fort Laramie Treaty – Lakota Sioux given Black Hills Dakota Generals Sherman/Sheridan angry
1869	Cross-USA railroad finished Promontory Point, Utah	Railroads advertised/sold land to homesteaders. More homesteaders	
1870	Cattle drives very common. Also more ranches on Plains		
1871	Beef sold on Plains to reservations, railroad builders		
1872	Gun laws and sheriffs reduced violence in cattle towns	Uriah Oblinger to Nebraska – typical homesteader	
1873		Mattie Oblinger and daughter to Nebraska. Thrilled to grow corn, etc.	
1874		**Typical homestead on Plains:** 'Sod' (earth) houses – unhealthy 1874 – Barbed wire: easier fencing Winter cold – burn dung 'chips' Summer droughts – wind pumps, and fenced-off water sources Lonely: church life helps Trade eggs and milk with neighbours Land very hard to plough Locusts could destroy crops	Gold miners into Black Hills Dakota Broke 1868 treaty Sitting Bull led Lakota Sioux resistance
1875			**Great Sioux War, 1875–77** Sitting Bull's vision of victory Crazy Horse joined Sitting Bull
1876			25 June – General Custer attacked at Little Big Horn. Had 210 cavalry Custer and all men killed Lakota Sioux on run. Crazy Horse arrested
1877			Crazy Horse killed – escape attempt? Full Lakota Sioux surrender. US took back Black Hills of Dakota – 40m acres.

> **Reflect**
> 1 What do the colour-coded sections have in common?
> 2 Why is this worth doing?

Method 5: Podcast – American cultures, 1877–1900

Some people like to listen to summaries of the main points. They find it helps them to remember key points. If you think this might work for you, make a podcast recording and play it back to yourself. You could do this by working with a friend to create an 'interview' style. If you were to do an interview about Enquiry 5, questions should cover, for example:

Changes for indigenous peoples	Changes for black Americans	Changes in business, cities and migration
• Defeat after Little Bighorn • Destruction of buffalo • Loss of land, water • Reservations: tribes split by government policy • Forced to farm – bad land • Had to depend on rations • Destruction of own culture: loss of language, customs, beliefs • 'Friends of Indian' • Dawes Act, 1887 • 'Wounded Knee' – Ghost Dancers' final resistance	• Free, but faced racism • Civil Rights campaigners, e.g. Ida Wells • In South, most were sharecroppers, very poor • Exodusters to Kansas, 1877 • In North, badly paid • Booker T. Washington: tried to help with schools, business • 'Jim Crow' laws in South • Black churches: important • 'Redeemer' governments in South: literacy test for voters • KKK in 1890s: lynchings	• Rise of business corporations, e.g. Carnegie and steel • Workers' wages kept low so many strikes • Big business methods in cotton, mining, ranching • Rise of cities: skyscrapers and slums. Health problems • Lively culture: parks, newspapers, entertainments • Mass migration to USA from Europe after 1880 • Symbol – Statue of Liberty • Racism against migrants

 Exam guidance

The World period study forms the first half of Paper 3. The whole exam lasts for 1 hour and 45 minutes. Allow just over 50 minutes to answer the four questions on the Making of America, 1789–1900.

Question 1

You will be asked three quick questions. Each is worth 1 mark. Questions begin, for example:

- 'Give one example of …'
- 'Name **one** …'
- 'Which …?'
- 'Name the …'
- 'What was …?'

Example

1   a   Name one of the states that was added to the USA between 1789 and 1838. (1)
    b   Name one of the US–Lakota Sioux wars fought between 1861 and 1876. (1)
    c   Name one of the main industries that provided employment for large numbers of black Americans in the South after 1877. (1)

Spend only one to two minutes on Question 1. Revise by making lots of cards. Each card should have a question on one side and at least one good, short answer on the back. Work with a friend. Use the cards to test each other.

Preparing for the examination

Question 2

This question is worth 9 marks. It will always begin like this: 'Write a clear and organised summary that analyses …'

You will be asked to write about an aspect of 'The Making of America, 1789–1900'. This will be a narrative account or a description.

Example

2 Write a clear and organised summary that analyses the difficulties faced by early colonists on their journeys to Oregon and California in the 1840s and 1850s. Support your summary with examples. (9)

Here are some important points to remember about Question 2:

- It is a summary. Do not go into too much detail. You should spend ten to twelve minutes on this question.
- Keep to the focus of the question. Watch out for date limits or particular issues you must address.
- It must use well-chosen, precise and accurate facts to support what you say.
- It must be clear and organised. Structure your answer:
  - If you want to make two or three main points, you probably need to write two or three short paragraphs.
  - You can write one long paragraph, but make sure your ideas flow in a sensible order and keep to the point.
- It must 'analyse' the issue in the question. As you write your answer, you should show understanding of a key historical idea like the ones that we used in the Key idea summaries after each enquiry. You do not need to name the 'key idea'. Just apply it in your answer.
- There is no single, right way to 'analyse' the issue. Here are two ways you could use a key historical idea to organise an answer to the example question shown above:

Analyse by diversity: different types of difficulty, e.g.	Analyse by cause: say what the difficulties were and why they existed, e.g.
• Climate/weather problems • Problems in the landscape: exposed Plains; high mountains • Disease and accident	• Bad planning: not enough food, leaving at a bad time year or getting isolated • Medical care not as good as we have today, even when not far from doctors • Some Native Americans grew hostile because migrant routes disturbed their buffalo hunting grounds

Question 3

This question is worth 10 marks. It will always ask you to explain your answer. The question will usually begin like this:

- 'Why …?'
- 'Why did …?'
- 'What was the impact of …?'
- 'What caused …?'
- 'Why do you think …?'

> **Example**
>
> 3 What was the impact of the California gold rush, 1848–49?
>   Explain your answer. (10)

Here are some important points to remember about Question 3:

- Spend about twelve to thirteen minutes on this question.
- Do not just list or describe events connected to the issue in the question. You must explain your answer.
- Use your first sentence to show that you have understood exactly what the question asks you to do.
- The question will very often be about *why* something happened. If so, explain the causes of the event. Here are some ways you could organise your causes:
  - Explain the most important causes first and the less important causes afterwards.
  - Explain 'long-term' causes first and 'short-term' causes afterwards.
  - Group some causes together in paragraphs, for example economic causes or religious causes.
- If the question is about 'impact', give examples of the consequences of the event. But that is not enough. You need to add an explanation as well. The table below shows two ways you might answer the example question shown above. It just shows outline plans. Your answer would need to add precise supporting details.

Explain how the California gold rush had *different effects for different groups*, e.g.	Explain *exactly how* the impact happened, e.g.
• California's population grew massively in just a year. This helped it to become a state in 1850. This led to pressure for a rail link across the USA • Miners had hoped to get rich but ended up working for mining companies • Native Americans, lost land and saw it polluted by mining activity	• California's population grew rapidly. This happened because … • Big mining companies took over the gold fields because … • Land and rivers became polluted because …

Preparing for the examination

Question 4/5

You must choose which of Question 4 or Question 5 you wish to answer. Whichever one you choose it is worth 18 marks. It is the most challenging question on this part of the examination.

The question will always ask you 'how far' you agree with a given statement. You must reach a clear judgement about this.

> ### Examples
>
> 4   How far do you agree that the building of railroads across the Plains was the main reason for the destruction of the indigenous peoples' culture after 1877? Give reasons for your answer. (18)
>
> 5   'The period of Reconstruction from 1863 to 1877 was a period of progress for people who had been freed from slavery in America's Southern states.' How far do you agree with this statement? Give reasons for your answer. (18)

Here are some important points about Questions 4 and 5.

- Spend about 25 minutes on this question.
- Watch out for dates in the question (e.g. question 4 above asks about the destruction of the indigenous peoples' culture *after* 1877).
- Remember to *reach a judgement* about the issue in the question. The question asks 'how far' you agree with a statement. You could strongly agree, strongly disagree or only just agree/disagree ... but do not sit on the fence!
- Whatever judgement you make, you must support it with clear understanding and precise knowledge.
- It helps to:
  - spend a short time thinking about the question and noting down points that you think are relevant
  - 'weigh up' the evidence in your notes, then decide on your judgement before you start to write your answer
  - write your judgement in your opening sentence
  - use the rest of the time to support your judgement.
- Always consider more than one side of the argument. The table below shows outline plans for the example questions shown above. Your answer would add precise details.

Q4: Railroads	Q5: Reconstruction
• Consider how railroads did help to destroy indigenous peoples' culture after 1877 • Consider other factors, e.g. ranches, homesteaders, US government policies, Dawes Act 1887 • Decide if railroads were the 'main' reason. State your judgement at the start	• Consider ways in which Reconstruction from 1863–77 did help people who had been freed from slavery • Consider ways in which Reconstruction failed to help ex-slaves and how early progress was lost • Decide if this was a period of progress. State your judgement at the start

Glossary

abolish ban, bring to an end

abolitionist a person who opposed slavery

academics highly educated people

Amendment to the Constitution of the USA a change to the Constitution of the USA

American Dream the hope of a better life which the USA could offer immigrants

Black Codes laws which discriminated against black Americans

Buffalo Dance a special dance to encourage the buffalo to return each year

capitalist (system) system which encourages individuals to make money for personal profit

caravan a group of travellers, often with wagons and horses

civil rights rights that people have as citizens of a country, affecting their daily lives

civil rights campaigners someone who fought for equal treatment of people

compromise a half-way deal where each person involved gets some but not all of what they want

Confederacy the name taken by the Southern states when they tried to break away from the Union and form their own nation

Confederates people who fought for the South during the Civil War

conflict a serious disagreement

Congress the name of the body that passes laws in the USA

constitution the rules by which a nation is governed

contrabands term used to describe enslaved people who had fled from their captors and worked for the Union army in the Civil War

convert change or turn around, often used to describe changes of religious belief

cotton gin a machine for separating cotton fibres

Cotton Kingdom the name given to the Deep South because of its links to cotton growing

cow towns towns set up for the buying and selling of cattle on railroads

culture a way of living shared by a group of people

Dawes Act a law which allowed people indigenous to the Great Plains to become citizens in return for giving up tribal claims to land

Declaration of Independence a document which split the American colonies from British rule

democracy a system in which decisions are made by voting

ecological something that tries not to cause lasting harm to the land or animal and plant life

Emancipation Proclamation a statement made on 1 January 1863 by President Lincoln that all enslaved people would be freed

Exodusters black settlers who moved to Kansas

exploitation taking advantage of someone or something without caring about the consequences

federal national, i.e. something that affects all the different states of the USA

fur trapper a person who hunted animals for fur and sold them for profit

Ghost Dancers Native Americans who lived on reservations and believed that white Americans could be removed from the Earth through a spiritual dance

Great Spirit one of the Lakota gods

Homestead Act a law passed in 1862 which promised 160 acres of land to anyone willing to work it for five years

homesteaders people who settled on the Plains

immigrant a person who moves to make a new home in a distant place

immigration the arrival of people from one place in another where they hope to stay and live

indigenous something or someone whose origins are deeply rooted in a place, e.g. Native Americans in America

invest give money to a business in return for a share of its profits each year

Jim Crow laws racist laws which attempted to reduce the power of black Americans

Ku Klux Klan a violent, racist, white supremacist group

Glossary

land speculators people who bought up land and sold it on for profits

Louisiana Purchase the name given to a deal in 1803 when France sold a huge area of land in North America to the USA

lynch to murder black people, often done by hanging them (a lynching)

Manifest Destiny a belief in a God-given right to take over the whole of America

migrant a person who moves from one place to another

migration the movement of people from one place to another

mission a group sent to convert people from one religion to another; it often provides health care or education for the people it tries to serve

Mormons followers of the teachings of Joseph Smith and the Book or Mormon

nomad person who lives by moving from place to place with no settled home

Plains (The Great Plains) the area of land between the Mississippi River and the Rocky Mountains

plantations large farms which grow a single crop, for example cotton

population the total number of people living in a particular place

prairies wide areas of grassland as found on the Plains

president (of the USA) the head of the American state, elected by voters every four years

pushing system a system in which enslaved people were forced to do more work than they had done before 1793

radical someone or something that attacks a problem by its roots rather than attempting minor changes

railroad the American term for what is called a railway in Britain

ranchers people who ran cattle ranches

Reconstruction the rebuilding of America after the Civil War

repeating rifles guns that could fire bullets rapidly one after another over long distances

reservation an area of land set aside for Native American settlement

resist stand up against, refuse to give in

secede to cut away from or leave

segregate divide, keep apart, e.g. black people from white people

Senate part of the USA's Congress where laws are made

Senators/Representatives people who are voted into Congress to represent their state

sharecroppers people who rented land by giving the landowner a share of their crops each year

slavery a system where some people own other people as property and put them to work

soddies houses made of earth

States (of America) different areas of the United States, each with its own government that must keep to the US Constitution

strike an event where all the workers in a particular workplace or industry stop working in order to demand better pay or conditions

Supreme Court the highest court in the USA that had to decide if new laws fitted the US Constitution

task system a system in which enslaved people were forced to complete a set number of tasks each day

territories name given to areas of land that were owned by the USA but not yet ready to become states

tipi a Plains peoples' name for a large tent

town boosters people who promoted the growth of their town and tried to encourage people to settle there

trade union a group of working people who work together to improve their pay and the conditions they work in

transcontinental something that crosses a whole continent, e.g. a railroad in the USA

treaty an official agreement between two nations, e.g. to end a war

Underground Railroad a secret organisation which helped enslaved people to escape to free states

Union a shorter name for the United States used by the Northern states in their war against the Confederacy

vision a way of looking at an issue or place

White League a racist, white supremacist group

World's Fair an exhibition in Chicago in 1893

yeoman farmer a self-sufficient landowner

Index

abolitionism 18, 47, 60
American Dream 93
Apache 28, 29
Arapaho 40–41, 74

Ball, Charles 24–25
big business 90–91
black Americans 7
    changes to way of life 86–89
    and Civil War 50–53
    and World's Fair 81
    see also slavery
Black Codes 55
Black Kettle 74
Bleeding Kansas 60
bonanza farms 91
Booth, John Wilkes 54
Bozeman Trail 75
Brown, John 60–61
Buchanan, James 48
buffalo 28–29
    destruction of 82
Buffalo Dance 29

California gold rush 38–39
California Trail 33, 38
Carnegie, Andrew 90
cattle ranching 63, 66, 67, 83, 91
Central Pacific Railroad Company 64
Cherokees 21, 22, 23
Cheyenne 28–29, 41, 74, 83
Chicago 80–81, 92, 93
Chickasaws 21
Chivington, John 74
Choctaws 21
cities, growth of 92–93
civil rights 56–57, 86
    Wells, Ida 86, 89
Civil War 44–54
    black Americans and 50–53
    causes of 46–9
    post-war reconstruction 54–58
Clay, Henry 47
coal industry 91
Comanche 94–95
Congress 7, 21, 47, 48, 56, 61
Constitution 7, 15, 89
    amendments 54, 56, 57
contrabands 51

cotton gin 16
cotton industry 14, 16, 17, 24–25, 46, 53, 87, 91
Cotton Kingdom 17
cotton plantations 15
cow towns 66–67
Crazy Horse 76, 77
Creeks 20, 21, 22
Custer, George Armstrong 76–77

Dakota (people) 63, 83
Davis, Jefferson 49
Dawes Act 84
Declaration of Independence 6
Democratic Party 48
Deslondes, Charles 18
Douglass, Frederick 47, 86
DuBois, William 88

Emancipation Proclamation 52
exam guidance 100–103
Exodusters 87

Fallen Timbers, Battle of 11
Five Civilised Tribes 21
Fort Laramie Treaty 35, 75, 76
Fort Pillow, Battle of 44
Freedman's Bureau 56, 58
Friends of the Indian 84
fur trade 13
fur trappers 26

Garrison, William Lloyd 47
Ghost Dancers 85
gold mining 38–41
Gooch, Nancy 38
Grant, Ulysses S. 57, 58
Greasy Grass (Little Bighorn), Battle of 76, 79
Great Sioux War 76
Greenville, Treaty of 11

Harper's Ferry attack 60
Hawkins, Benjamin 21
He Sapa (Black Hills), Dakota 29, 31, 75, 76, 77
Homestead Act 68
homesteaders 65, 68–71, 83

Iliff, John 67
immigration 93
Indian Removal Act 21

Jackson, Andrew 19, 21, 22
Jefferson, Thomas 12, 13, 16
Jim Crow laws 88
Johnson, Andrew 55, 56, 57

Kansas–Nebraska Act 48
Ku Klux Klan 58, 59, 89

Lakota Sioux 29–31, 35, 75–77, 83
land speculators 13, 19
Lee, John D. 37
Lewis and Clark 10, 13
Lincoln, Abraham 44, 48, 49, 51, 52, 54, 64
Little Crow's War 73
Louisiana Purchase 13, 17
lynching 53, 89

McCoy, Joseph 67
Manifest Destiny 32, 62
migrants to Far West 32–35
Miller, Alfred Jacob 26, 28
mind maps 98–99
mining industry
    coal mining 91
    gold mining 38–41
Missouri Compromise 17, 48
Mormons 36–37, 43
mountain men 26–27, 32–33

National Anti-Slavery Society 47
Native Americans. 7, 11, 32, 41
    changes in way of life 82–85
    expulsion of 20–23
    and gold mining 39
    and migrants 35
    Plains tribes 28–31, 72–77, 82, 83, 84, 85
        culture, destruction of 84
        Ghost Dancers 85
        railroads 40, 64–65
        reservations 72, 73, 82, 83
    World's Fair 81
North/South divide 46, 50
    religious/political differences 15, 48
    see also Civil War; slavery
Northwest Territory 11, 12, 15, 20

Index

Oblinger family 69, 71
Oregon Trail 33, 34
O'Sullivan, John 62

Palmer, Frances 62–63
Parker, Quanah 94–95
Pike's Peak gold rush 40–41
Plains 62–79
    cattle ranching 63, 66, 67, 91
    homesteaders 65, 68–71
Plains tribes 28–31, 72–77, 82, 83, 84, 85
    culture, destruction of 84
    Ghost Dancers 85
    railroads 40, 64–65
    reservations 72, 73, 82, 83
presidential office 7
Pullman strike 90

railroads 40, 64–65, 68, 95

Red Cloud 75–76
Red Cloud's War 75
Redeemers 89
Republican Party 48
Roosevelt, Theodore 94

Sager family 34
Salt Lake City 36–37
Sand Creek Massacre 74
Scott, Abigail 42–43
Seminole people 20, 21
Seminole wars 22
sharecroppers 58
Sherman, General 53, 75
Singleton, Benjamin 87
Sitting Bull 76, 77, 82, 85
slave auctions 19, 17
slavery 7, 14, 15, 16–19, 24–25, 46
    abolitionism 18, 47, 60
    abolition of 54
    Emancipation Proclamation 52
    growth of 16–17
Smith, Joseph 36
Southwest Territory 11, 12, 15, 20
state system 7
Stowe, Harriet Beecher 47
Strauss, Levi 38
Supreme Court 7, 59

Taylor, Susie King 53
territories 7, 37
timelines 99
tobacco industry 14, 91
Trail of Tears 23
Tubman, Harriet 47, 51, 53
Turner, Nat 24

Underground Railroad 47
Union Pacific Company 64

War of Independence 11
Washington, Booker T. 87
Washington, George 6, 11
Wells, Ida 86, 89
white Americans 7, 12, 72
White League 58, 59
Whitman Mission 34
Whitney, Eli 16
World's Fair, Chicago 81
Wounded Knee massacre 85

Yakima treaty 35
yeoman farmers 12
Young, Brigham 36, 37

Acknowledgements

Text acknowledgements

p.24 Edward E. Baptist, *The Half Has Never Been Told: Slavery and the Making of American Capitalism*. New York: Basic Books, 2014; **p.42** Abigail Scott's diary, http://cateweb.uoregon.edu/duniway/notes/DiaryProof1.html

Picture credits

p.6 © Granger Historical Picture Archive/Alamy Stock Photo; **pp.8–9, p.4** © Danita Delimont/Alamy Stock Photo; **p.11, p.4** © Chicago History Museum/Getty Images; **p.12, p.4** © Everett Historical/Shutterstock; **p.13, p.4** © Granger Historical Picture Archive/Alamy Stock Photo; **p.14** © AF Fotografie/Alamy Stock Photo; **p.16** © Granger Historical Picture Archive/Alamy Stock Photo; **p.17** The Historic New Orleans Collection, acc. no. 1940.4; **p.19** © ClassicStock/Alamy Stock Photo; **p.21** *t* © Granger Historical Picture Archive/Alamy Stock Photo, *b* © Everett Collection Historical/Alamy Stock Photo; **p.23, p.5** © Woolaroc Museum, Bartlesville, Oklahoma; **p.24, p.5** © World History Archive/Alamy Stock Photo; **p.26** © Walters Art Museum/https://creativecommons.org/publicdomain/zero/1.0/; **p.28** © Walters Art Museum/https://creativecommons.org/publicdomain/zero/1.0/; **p.29** © Paul Mellon Collection, National Gallery of Art Washington; **p.30** © Herbert Orth/The LIFE Images Collection/Getty Images; **p.31** © Peter Newark Western Americana; American/Bridgeman Images; **p.32** © Library of Congress Prints and Photographs Division, LC-USZC4-2744; **p.34** © Hulton Archive/Getty Images; **p.36** © Library of Congress Prints and Photographs Division, LC-BH82-4714; **p.37** © Fotosearch/Getty Images; **p.38** © Popperfoto/Getty Images; **p.39** © Library of Congress Prints and Photographs Division, Washington, LC-DIG-pga-01463; **p.40** © Nebraska State Historical Society, RG1576.PH-02; **p.42** *t* © Library of Congress Prints and Photographs Division Washington/LC-USZ61-787, *b* © MPI/Getty Images; **p.44** © Peter Newark American Pictures/Bridgeman Images; **p.47** © GL Archive/Alamy Stock Photo; **p.48** © Niday Picture Library/Alamy Stock Photo; **p.49** © Library of Congress Prints and Photographs Division, LC-DIG-ppmsca-19520; **p.50** *l* © Dorling Kindersley ltd/Alamy Stock Photo, *r* © E + I/Getty Images; **p.51** *t* © Library of Congress Prints and Photographs Division Washington, LC-DIG-ds-05120, *b* © Library of Congress Prints and Photographs Division, LC-USZ62-7816; **p.52** © Z4 Collection/Alamy Stock Photo; **p.53** *t* © Library of Congress Prints and Photographs Division, LC-DIG-ppmsca-11128, *b* © Granger Historical Picture Archive/Alamy Stock Photo; **p.54** © Library of Congress Prints and Photographs Division Washington, LC-USZ61-1938; **p.55** © North Wind Picture Archives/Alamy Stock Photo; **p.57** © Library of Congress Prints and Photographs Division Washington, LC-DIG-ppmsca-30572; **p.58** © North Wind Picture Archives/Alamy Stock Photo; **p.59** © Library of Congress Prints and Photographs Division Washington, LC-USZ62-128619; **p.60** © National Portrait Gallery, Washington; **p.62** © Akademie/Alamy Stock Photo; **p.64** © Granger Historical Picture Archive/Alamy Stock Photo; **p.65** © Kansas Collection, Spencer Research Library, Universities of Kansas Libraries; **p.66** © Arco Images GmbH/Alamy Stock Photo; **p.67** © Bettmann/Getty Images; **p.68** © Kansas State Historical Society; **p.69** © Nebraska State Historical Society, RG1346-1-2; **pp.70–71** © Nebraska State Historical Society, RG-2608.PH-1425; **p.73** *t* © Library of Congress Prints and Photographs Division, LC-USZ61-83, *b* © GL Archive/Alamy Stock Photo; **p.74** © Allen Memorial Art Museum, Oberlin College, Ohio, USA/Gift of Mrs. Jacob D. Cox/Bridgeman Images; **p.75** © Granger Historical Picture Archive/Alamy Stock Photo; **p.76** *t* © IanDagnall Computing/Alamy Stock Photo, *b* © Library of Congress Prints and Photographs Division, LC-B813-1613 A; **p.77** © a-plus image bank/Alamy Stock Photo; **p.78** © GraphicaArtis/Getty Images; **p.80** © Chicago History Museum/Getty Images; **p.81** North Wind Picture Archives/Alamy Stock Photo; **p.82** © Hi-Story/Alamy Stock Photo; **p.83** © John Alvin Anderson/Library of Congress/Corbis/VCG via Getty Images; **p.84** *l* © Granger Historical Picture Archive/Alamy Stock Photo, *r* © Granger Historical Picture Archive/Alamy Stock Photo; **p.86** Public domain/https://en.wikipedia.org/wiki/File:Mary_Garrity_-_Ida_B._Wells-Barnett_-_Google_Art_Project_-_restoration_crop.jpg; **p.87** *t* © Granger Historical Picture Archive/Alamy Stock Photo, *b* © Library of Congress Prints and Photographs Division, LC-DIG-hec-16114; **p.88** © Archive Photos/Getty Images; **p.90** *t* © Stocktrek Images/Getty Images; *b* © Library of Congress Prints and Photographs Division Washington, LC-USZC4-3108; **p.92** © Chronicle/Alamy Stock Photo; **p.93** © PVDE/Bridgeman Images; **p.94** © Granger Historical Picture Archive/Alamy Stock Photo